"*End Emotional Eating* may be the beginning for you in a new relationship with food and your feelings. Who hasn't had a craving for food that came from a sense of emptiness, anxiety, or anger? This book is filled with powerful metaphors, empowering messages, and mental and emotional exercises that will keep you from eating away at your feelings. Accessible, intelligent, and compassionate, this book can help you find a new way of experiencing and using emotions. You will find wisdom that you can use every day. I highly recommend this book."

—Robert L. Leahy, PhD, founder and director of the American Institute for Cognitive Therapy, professor at Weill Cornell Medical College and NewYork-Presbyterian Hospital, and past president of the Association for Behavioral and Cognitive Therapies.

"If you struggle with emotional eating and want to end the battle, this is the place to start. Based on solid scientific evidence, the author offers carefully selected, elegantly described, bite-sized techniques to release oneself from every aspect of the emotional eating cycle. The author did the work for us in this impressive, comprehensive work, and now we just need to begin. I highly recommend this book to anyone who seeks freedom from unhealthy eating habits and those who care for them."

—Christopher Germer, PhD, author of *The Mindful Path to Self-Compassion* and clinical instructor at Harvard Medical School

"It's a pleasure to see a book with a genuinely new perspective to offer the countless individuals who struggle and suffer over the simple daily act of eating. Well-grounded in scientific research, yet also written in a lively, accessible manner with moving personal stories and plenty of specific, explicit, practical advice, Jennifer L. Taitz offers plenty of new food for thought about food. This will be a helpful and valuable read for anyone who has let his or her eating be guided more by emotion than nutrition."

—Roy F. Baumeister, PhD, author of *Willpower: Rediscovering the Greatest Human Strength*

P9-COO-853

"I have spent my entire career educating people about what to eat to maintain a healthy weight. But if there is one thing I have learned, it is that most people who struggle with their weight are not simply hungrier than their thinner peers. They eat for reasons other than hunger: sadness, loneliness, anger, and frustration. Emotional eating is often at the core of the poor choices people make when it comes to food. Jennifer L. Taitz has made a major contribution to helping those who suffer from emotional eating. She identifies the basic emotions that give rise to unhealthy eating habits and offers readers the skills and tools to end emotional eating once and for all."

> —Tanya Zuckerbrot, MS, RD, founder of F-Factor and author of *The F-Factor Diet*

"Why do we eat? Seems obvious, right? —Because we have to eat to stay alive! But many of us eat to feel better. We eat to push away feelings of anxiety, sadness, and self-loathing. Jennifer L. Taitz can help us stop. Her book, *End Emotional Eating*, helps us understand the link between emotions and eating. More importantly, it helps us break those links so that we have more healthy ways to regulate our emotions and so that our eating is not driven by our emotional state. The strategies taught in this book are innovative and powerful, and they have been shown to truly help people end emotional eating."

> —Susan Nolen-Hoeksema, PhD, professor of psychology at Yale University and author of *Women Who Think Too Much* and *Eating, Drinking, Overthinking*

"Jennifer L. Taitz's insight, compassion, and far-reaching clinical experience shine from every page."

> —Sharon Salzberg, author of *Real Happiness: The Power of Meditation*

"Dialectical behavior therapy (DBT) is an effective treatment for a variety of psychological disorders. Never before has the wisdom of DBT, as it applies to emotional eating, been so clearly articulated. Authored by a master clinician and talented writer, this book artfully describes how to transform your relationship with food and life. I highly recommend that you read this book if you want to gain a new perspective on your emotional reactions and change the way you think about and respond to impulses to eat. This is not a diet book; it is a book that will provide nourishment for your soul and psyche. A genuine treat!"

> —Dennis Greenberger, PhD, director of the Anxiety and Depression Center in Newport Beach, CA, and coauthor of *Mind Over Mood*

"This is not a weight loss book. It is something much, much better. If you have tried over and over to control your weight and your eating, maybe it is time to let go of that agenda. This is a book about changing your fundamental relationship with food and eating, and importantly, your relationship to yourself! Imagine that you could come into a gentler, more compassionate relationship with yourself and with eating. If you want to explore a kinder approach, this is the book for you."

> —Kelly G. Wilson, PhD, cofounder of acceptance and commitment therapy and associate professor at the University of Mississippi

"Highly recommended. *End Emotional Eating* provides a sensitive and thoughtful account of how emotions and eating become entangled in a multitude of unhelpful ways, together with clear guidance for unraveling them and moving forward using a blend of ancient and modern approaches."

> —Christopher G. Fairburn, MD, professor of psychiatry at the University of Oxford and author of *Overcoming Binge Eating*

end

emotional

EATING

USING

DIALECTICAL BEHAVIOR

THERAPY SKILLS TO

Cope with Difficult

Emotions and Develop a

Healthy Relationship

to Food

JENNIFER L. TAITZ, PSYD

NEW HARBINGER PUBLICATIONS, INC.

Publisher's Note

Distributed in Canada by Raincoast Books

Copyright © 2012 by Jennifer L. Taitz
New Harbinger Publications, Inc.
5674 Shattuck Avenue
Oakland, CA 94609
www.newharbinger.com

All Rights Reserved

Acquired by Melissa Kirk; Cover design by Amy Shoup; Edited by Clancy Drake

Library of Congress Cataloging-in-Publication Data

Taitz, Jennifer.
  End emotional eating : using dialectical behavior therapy skills to cope with difficult emotions and develop a healthy relationship to food / Jennifer Taitz.
     p. cm.
  Summary: "Dialectical behavior therapy (DBT) expert and clinical psychologist Jenny Taitz presents End Emotional Eating, a comprehensive guide to overcoming the emotional eating issues that are at the root of most overeating and binge eating difficulties"-- Provided by publisher.
  Includes bibliographical references.
  ISBN 978-1-60882-121-1 (pbk.) -- ISBN 978-1-60882-122-8 (pdf e-book) -- ISBN 978-1-60882-123-5 (epub)
  1. Eating disorders--Treatment. 2. Dialectical behavior therapy. I. Title.
  RC552.E18.T35 2012
  616.85'26--dc23
                          2012008372

Printed in the United States of America

17 16 15

10 9 8 7 6 5

CONTENTS

ACKNOWLEDGMENTS

I thank divine grace for the sequence of events resulting in this moment. With gratitude and sadness, I honor the memory of my maternal grandparents, Emil and Sylvia "Ceiba" Seletz. What a blessing just to meet humans like them, let alone have them in my family. From my birth until their death they showed me unparalleled adoration. My grandma was a model of selfless love and generosity. My grandpa was a neurosurgeon and accomplished sculptor who taught me that patience and precision matter most. As I matured I dreamed of finding a path on which I could emulate his manner of healing mental difficulties using science and wit; this eventually led me to pursue training in clinical psychology. My grandma and grandpa made people many would not notice feel as though they were Nobel Prize winners and showed me that loving and learning matter more than all else.

My parents have generously raised and supported me and were kind enough to encourage me when I announced I would write a book. My mother, Jo, has modeled that a woman may embrace her career and also live fully. My father, Emanuel, told me that if I am passionate about something, I will find success. I feel lucky to have people in my life who take my dreams seriously!

I extend a lot of love and thanks to my sisters, Michelle, who was aptly critical on edits and often hospitable with dinner invitations during this process, and Rebecca; my aunt, Sonia Taitz, a brilliant and funny author who kindly edited a lot of this book; my uncle Paul; my uncle Jimmy; and my paternal grandparents, Simon and Gita, courageous Holocaust survivors who lived purposefully. Kate Ballen feels like family and is a generous friend and talented author.

I experienced the clinical psychology equivalent of winning the lottery when I met Dennis Tirch and began my long-standing collaboration working with him and Robert Leahy at the American Institute for Cognitive Therapy (AICT) in New York City. AICT is an internationally known practice and training institute where advances in CBT are discussed and used therapeutically.

I would like to thank the following influential thinkers: Marsha Linehan, Aaron Beck, Sharon Salzberg, Debra Safer, Christopher Fairburn, Steven Hayes, Daniel Gilbert, Roy Baumeister, Zindel Segal, Susan Nolen-Hoeksema, and the countless others whose wisdom I simply organized in the pages ahead.

I am enormously grateful to Melissa Kirk, Jess Beebe, Nicola Skidmore, Clancy Drake, and all of the people at New Harbinger who offered me this opportunity and provided pointed direction.

The following people have been both friends and mentors: Batya Rotter, Ana Benitez, Geoff Platt, Tova Gozdzik, Lisa Napolitano, Simon Rego, Ilyse Dobrow Dimarco, Jonathan Kaplan, Laura Oliff, Danielle Kaplan, Annalise Caron, Dennis Greenberger, Kelly Wilson, John Forsyth, Josh Pretsky, Dan Goodman, Linda Dimeff, Rene Zweig, Lata McGinn, Irma Hilton, Kelly Riley, and Poonam Melwani.

Balancing and binding postures in yoga continuously help me cultivate perspective, stamina, patience, and balance and experientially introduced me to the mental elements I label today as "mindfulness" and "acceptance." I thank my many teachers, including Steve Ross and Scott Harig. I have learned a lot about living according to my values from my many spiritual influences, including the Adler family, Judy Millman, Yehuda Sarna, and Shlomo Einhorn.

I acknowledge my wonderfully inspiring patients, and you, the reader, for allowing me to move a bit closer to what really matters to me.

FOREWORD

*O*ver the past two decades, the emergence of the third wave of behavioral therapies has resulted in new, empirically supported treatments such as dialectical behavior therapy (Linehan 1993a, 1993b), acceptance and commitment therapy (Hayes, Strosahl, and Wilson 1999), and mindfulness-based cognitive therapy (Segal, Williams, and Teasdale 2002). These therapeutic approaches expand upon earlier treatments. The second-wave therapies (such as cognitive behavioral therapy) added to the first-wave therapies (such as behavioral therapy) by calling attention to the role of cognitions. The third-wave treatments then added a metacognitive component, an awareness of thinking itself. These treatments emphasize the development of mindfulness, or the ability to experience the present moment with nonjudgmental awareness.

In *End Emotional Eating*, Dr. Jennifer Taitz clearly introduces key concepts and principles from these recently developed treatments, including adaptations that have been made specifically for individuals with eating disorders. The text further offers useful and easy-to-understand exercises taken from these therapies, so individuals struggling with emotional eating can readily benefit from them. This may lead to decisions to initiate treatment with local practitioners who have been trained to deliver these therapies—an especially important consideration for those with serious eating disturbances. Others might choose to share the book with their therapists to work on some of the proposed exercises together. As a clinical investigator and psychotherapist applying dialectical behavior therapy for binge eating disorder and bulimia, I appreciate Dr. Taitz giving clinicians such a useful, thoughtful, and easy-to-read resource that provides therapists and clients with a deeper understanding of often difficult-to-convey concepts from the expanding field of eating disorder treatments.

What individuals suffering from emotional eating—or clinicians treating these disorders—will find so inviting about *End Emotional Eating* is how accessible it is as a guide to dialectical behavior therapy, acceptance and commitment therapy, and mindfulness-based cognitive therapy. For example, not only does Dr. Taitz explain fundamental concepts in comprehensible terms, but she also adds personal anecdotes—such as sharing her experience during a five-day "silent" meditation retreat led by Dr. Marsha Linehan in which a short exchange with Dr. Linehan led to significant shifts in Dr. Taitz's own understanding of mindfulness. In addition, Dr. Taitz culled through a considerable research literature to introduce readers to some of the most exciting and pertinent studies that support the theoretical implications of the third-wave behavior therapies. She makes use of her extensive clinical experience working with individuals struggling with food to offer many practical and effective exercises.

In short, I found myself engrossed in Dr. Taitz's *End Emotional Eating*, and I believe it will be extremely useful to those wishing for a very clearly written discussion of the latest empirically supported therapies and their application for the treatment of eating disorders.

—Debra L. Safer, MD
   Author, *Dialectical Behavior Therapy for Binge Eating and Bulimia*
   Co-Director of the Stanford Adult Eating and Weight
      Disorders Program
   Assistant Professor, Department of Psychiatry and
      Behavioral Sciences
   Stanford University School of Medicine

Introduction

MARSHMALLOWS AND MINDFULNESS

What do marshmallows teach us about mindfulness—a quality of awareness that facilitates living flexibly? In a landmark study at Stanford University, four-year-olds at Bing, the school's research nursery school, were offered a marshmallow. They were told they could either eat the marshmallow immediately or wait. If they waited to eat the marshmallow that sat before their eyes until the experimenter returned (about 15 minutes), they would receive two marshmallows.

Walter Mischel, a psychologist studying delaying gratification, had three daughters who attended Bing; they and their classmates participated in the study. Over the years, he would ask his daughters about their friends, and in doing so he detected a relationship between an ability to delay gratification in preschool and excelling in adolescence. Mischel and his colleagues located the participants in the initial study to more formally track their progress as they matured (1989). They noticed that the children who ate the single marshmallow right away were likely to have problems in the areas of behavior, friendships, and attention. In contrast, those who were able to delay gratification had higher SAT scores and coped better with stress. This study addresses the question of whether self-control is a skill we can learn.

Willpower, as it turns out, is less about will than it is about skill. Mischel explains that willpower relates to the ability to strategically direct attention. For example, teaching children to pretend the marshmallow is just a picture transforms low delayers to high delayers. Obsessing and focusing on the marshmallow creates intense temptation, while bringing attention to other factors or thoughts—covering the marshmallow or singing Sesame Street songs—facilitates waiting (cited in Lehrer 2009).

In this book, you will learn to sit with temptation by paying attention in a particular way. You will become able to cultivate habits that matter to you. When you modify the ways you participate in a given moment, you increase your ability to move away from obsessing over food, toward the larger reward of eating and living wisely.

I would genuinely like to thank you for having the courage to pick up this book. It takes strength to explore new ways to handle feelings and eating habits. In the short term, it may feel easier to avoid the challenge of changing our habits, even if we know deep down that our efforts to avoid change will only make things worse. Challenges seldom resolve themselves, and even though you may have explored various solutions, you're willing to try something new by reading and working through this book.

If you struggle to live fully and joyously because of an unhealthy relationship with eating, my hope is that this book will offer you new freedom. Eating is a part of life, and this book is about living in a way that is meaningful and expansive. Unlike hundreds of other books, it will not tell you what, when, how, or how much to eat. Instead, you will practice living in full contact with the present moment, learning from your feelings, coping with distress skillfully, and developing self-compassion. These practices build a powerful foundation for making choices about food that are loving, joyous, and healthful.

Who Is This Book For?

We face food constantly. It is a fact of life: food nourishes our body and fuels our mind. However, many of us have the experience that what sustains us may also diminish us and engender a sense of shame and anxiety. Perhaps you have noticed yourself eating without feeling particularly hungry, a behavior that may stem from eating in response to emotions. *Emotional eating*, eating in response to an emotion rather than a physiological need, may quell boredom or stress and offer a sense of comfort in the short term. However, when we come to rely on food to cope with difficult feelings, it can interfere with our ability to use healthier methods of both learning from and dealing with feelings—it keeps us from uncovering our personal potential. Beyond this, such use of food can actually lead to our feeling worse, both physically and emotionally. If you've ever noticed yourself eating when—and because—you're bored, anxious, lonely, happy, or sad, this book will help you increase your awareness and acceptance of the emotions you experience without needing food to help you cope with them. Over time, weakening the link between food and short-term emotional consolation can allow you to gradually cultivate healthier and more sustaining ways of responding to your emotions. And it can help you experience food in the most nourishing, nurturing, and satisfying ways.

This book may serve as a companion to traditional weight-loss methods, including weight loss books. However, this is not a diet book, nor is it even exclusively for people who want to lose weight. Instead it aims to address the psychological aspects of eating and food obsessing that are not typically touched upon in conventional weight-loss books.

If you have an eating disorder (we'll review eating disorders in chapter 1), this book is not an alternative to comprehensive treatment. Once you are already in treatment with a professional, however, this book may serve as a useful addition to your therapy. Whether you struggle with weight, overfocus on food, or obsess about your body, *End Emotional Eating* will help you deepen and broaden your life's focus.

End Emotional Eating will introduce you to the latest tools found in clinical and research psychology to help you manage emotions in a way that lets you live in the present. If you are afraid of or uncomfortable with emotions and find yourself trying to suppress them, this book will provide you with practical skills to navigate them. After all, there is no alternative: living means feeling.

Mindfulness and Acceptance

Let's begin with the most important concepts in this book: mindfulness and acceptance. *Mindfulness* describes present-moment-focused, flexible, nonjudgmental awareness. It's about experiencing the reality of where you are now, rather than living in the abstractions of your thoughts about the past or future. *Acceptance* means a willingness to experience thoughts and feelings, even uncomfortable ones. It doesn't mean endorsing things we don't want to experience or running headlong into unpleasantness. When we practice acceptance, it means that we acknowledge the reality of our life's circumstances, and we make space for the flow of the whole of our inner world, without needlessly trying to defend ourselves against it or escape it. We will spend a lot of time in later chapters exploring these concepts.

More and more research has established that these principles, more than anything else you can try (or have perhaps already tried), will change your relationship with difficult experiences. By the way, many people assume that acceptance is the antithesis of change. Not so. As you will come to see, acceptance describes a stance that gracefully precedes, and escorts, change.

What comes to mind when you hear the words "mindfulness and acceptance"? Some people assume these ideas to be simplistic and insufficient for significant problems. They may lump mindfulness and acceptance into a "New Age"/ "not for me" category. I urge you to notice any judgments that arise—favorable, unfavorable, or neutral—and hold them lightly, not buying into anything (or rejecting anything) until you fully experiment with these life stances.

Strategies Used in This Book

Many of the concepts we will explore in this book originate from scientifically supported therapies, which I will outline below. I don't want to confuse you with acronyms (or alphabet soup), but my main intention is to let you know that the concepts in this book are not based on whim or on my thoughts alone. These approaches are considered to be the latest advances in cognitive behavioral therapy (CBT) and have been found helpful in randomized controlled trials for a wide range of problems. In this book I'll present concepts and practices from three main modes of treatment.

Dialectical Behavior Therapy (DBT)

Marsha Linehan, a professor at the University of Washington, developed dialectical behavior therapy (DBT) to teach people how to manage emotions that feel overwhelming (1993a, 1993b). She noticed that pushing people to change wasn't as effective as teaching people to both change and accept at the same time. This treatment synthesized elements from her years as both a behavioral therapist and a student in the Zen tradition.

Some people experience emotions more deeply than others. If you have never been taught how to accept or attend to your feelings, you may also experience emotions more intensely. DBT has taught thousands of people around the world how accepting emotions can help regulate emotions. If you find that your emotions operate almost like a light switch with "on" and "off" positions, DBT will help you learn to modulate your feelings, as a dimmer might better control the lighting in a room. Briefly, DBT will teach you practical skills, including the following (Linehan 1993a, 1993b):

- *Mindfulness:* A "core" DBT skill, mindfulness involves being in the moment and thinking nonjudgmentally in order to experience freedom and participate in life.

- *Emotion regulation:* This skill involves learning the function of emotions and improves your ability to describe, change, and cope effectively with them, rather than letting them control you.

- *Distress tolerance:* Distress tolerance is an ability to manage crises without making problems worse.

- *Interpersonal effectiveness:* Interpersonal effectiveness allows you to attend to your own needs and improve your relationships.

Originally, DBT was created to help individuals prone to self-harming and suicidal behavior due to emotional pain. Many world-renowned psychiatric hospitals now teach DBT to their patients. Studies comparing DBT to other reputable treatments have found DBT to be helpful in treating individuals who struggle with difficult emotions, self-harm, binge eating, bulimia, and depression (e.g., Linehan 1993a; Telch, Agras, and Linehan 2001; Wisniewski, Safer, and Chen 2007; Lynch, Mendelson, and Robins 2003). DBT has also been used to address marital difficulties (Fruzzetti 2006). In my clinical practice, I teach elements from DBT when appropriate even to people who do not have notable difficulties with emotions but who want to live more effectively; these clients invariably remark on how beneficial they find DBT skills.

Acceptance and Commitment Therapy (ACT)

ACT is a treatment developed by Steven Hayes at the University of Nevada, Reno, and his colleagues Kirk Strosahl and Kelly Wilson. ACT teaches people to become psychologically flexible, to let go of rigid patterns, and to build a life they choose, rather than a life based on avoiding or fighting their feelings. ACT is about allowing yourself to experience negative emotions if they arise while you are moving toward what matters to you. Many unwanted experiences, including thoughts and feelings, can't be controlled, but you can still commit to actions that keep you living in line with your personal values. Like DBT, ACT has been researched extensively and has been found remarkably helpful in treating a wide range of psychological problems. Recently, ACT has increasingly been applied in the area of body image and eating (Forman et al. 2009; Pearson, Heffner, and Follette 2010; Sandoz, Wilson, and DuFrene 2011).

Mindfulness-Based Cognitive Therapy (MBCT)

MBCT is a program developed by Zindel Segal at the University of Toronto and his colleagues Mark Williams and John Teasdale (2002). The treatment is strongly influenced by Jon Kabat-Zinn's mindfulness-based stress reduction (MBSR) program (1990), and it teaches people to practice mindfulness to get out of repetitive, distressing mental loops, which are common in people who suffer from depression. After completing MBCT treatment, participants have been shown to drastically reduce their risk of falling back into an episode of depression (Segal, Williams, and Teasdale 2002). In fact, MBCT is as effective as an antidepressant medication in preventing relapse (Segal et al. 2010). You might think of mindfulness as a medicine you can create through mental exercises.

Often, people who struggle with emotions and eating tend to get stuck in mental loops of painful thoughts that create and exacerbate distressing feelings. Many people who worry a lot about eating fluctuate between obsessing around food and body size and eating mindlessly. Mindfulness has been found helpful in the treatment of problems with emotions and eating in that it facilitates sitting with an emotion in a way that short-circuits these cycles of distress and distorted thinking (Baer, Fischer, and Huss 2005).

In this book, I will weave together the philosophical underpinnings of these three styles of treatment with practical exercises, teaching the cultivation of compassion and wisdom as a means of ending emotional eating.

A Little about Me

I'm originally from Los Angeles and have spent many years living in New York City. Since childhood, I have observed our culture's preoccupation with weight and shape. It was all around me—classmates of mine in the third grade experimented with the cabbage soup diet. I've also been infiltrated with messages about the importance of stopping bad feelings and trying to feel good at all times. We seem to live in a "birthday or wake, let's eat cake" culture—and we all have thoughts and feelings and are vulnerable. Like so many people, I am familiar with the experience of feeling imperfect and flawed—and of trying, usually ineffectively, to hide this sense.

In my adult life, I have learned to practice mindfulness and acceptance skills and have found them to be enormously helpful in tempering the strength and sway of these feelings of imperfection, worry, and shame. I first tasted what I now call "mindfulness" and "acceptance" as a young adult within the context of yoga. Then I began to understand these practices within a scientific context in my studies in psychology. In my early training experiences, I worked with numerous clients and various therapeutic styles, even working with incarcerated populations. Initially, I felt sickened by the pessimism I perceived in the field; it was difficult for me to accept the bleakness of certain prognoses. I much preferred the idea of wholeheartedly sitting with others with hope—especially hope for relief from conditions other professionals in my field deemed hopeless.

Mindfulness and acceptance, rooted in compassion, aligned with my personal values and strong optimism.

I studied DBT extensively, undertaking intensive training in DBT, completing a fellowship in DBT at Yale University School of Medicine, and directing the American Institute for Cognitive Therapy's DBT program. More recently, I have studied and treated clients using ACT and MBCT as well. I'm really enthusiastic about mindfulness- and acceptance-based treatments because I've seen them work—including for people who insisted nothing would work.

Many of my patients who struggle with intense emotions, including anxiety and depression, also struggle with eating problems. Many of them really suffer around food, and it pulls at my heart, because although food is something we can't live without, too little or too much can be fatal. I know many people who put their lives on hold as a result of problems with eating, and I see how this can really thwart their ability to participate fully in life. We can wait a long time for our circumstances to change, meanwhile missing opportunities (and feeling worse and eating worse). Or we can pick up new tools that will allow us to move forward.

What Lies Ahead

This book introduces concepts of mindfulness and acceptance. I will show you some practical tools for using these concepts to understand and manage your emotions, eating, and ways of coping with urges. In later chapters, I'll broaden the focus from managing feelings and eating to building a life that matters, addressing self-compassion and finding meaning in life.

In the pages ahead, you'll encounter a lot of material, which will provide you with a range of choices. Each person is unique, so explore the various tools and experiment with what resonates with you. This will come alive when you apply what's here, rather than merely reading. It may be useful to keep a journal in which you write notes, answer thought-provoking questions, and keep track of the exercises you've practiced and your observations on them. I spent many years thinking that mindfulness seemed like a good idea and practicing it sporadically. I found that, as with most experiences, there is a relationship between investment and return. With routine, repetitive commitment, I have experienced greater rewards.

I also notice that regular practice is often more helpful than massed practice. In other words, eating one meal mindfully each day and accepting difficult feelings each day for ten minutes at work can generate greater rewards than sitting mindfully for three hours once a week.

Notice your experience as you practice moving toward mindfulness and acceptance. It may be useful to set up practice commitments or appointments with yourself each day to eat one meal mindfully and practice accepting emotions in a specific situation. Take note of what has helped you follow through with new habits. Often, setting specific, feasible steps is very important. If you'd like a friendly reminder each day, Habit Forge (habitforge.com) will send you e-mails for three weeks reminding you to keep up with the goal of your choice. You may also enlist a willing friend to join you in sharing mindfulness observations along the way. The website stickK.com is another helpful tool to facilitate goals. The site allows you to create behavioral commitments and choose what's at stake if you don't follow through.

I find it helpful to remind myself that there is no trying: it's doing or not doing. My hope is that this book and, more importantly, your experiential practices in mindfulness and acceptance will pave for you a path of joy, compassion, and balance. And allow you to fully and patiently savor a marshmallow.

chapter 1

UNDERSTANDING
EMOTIONS AND EATING

People have a hard time letting go of their suffering. Out of
a fear of the unknown, they prefer suffering that is familiar.

—THICH NHAT HANH

In 1978, psychologists studying happiness examined Illinois state lottery winners and also victims of devastating accidents, some of whom
were left paralyzed from the neck down (Brickman, Coates, and
Janoff-Bulman). A control group of people randomly selected from the
phone book also participated. The researchers asked the participants
questions about their levels of past happiness, current happiness, and
anticipated future happiness. Individuals from each group were also asked
how much they enjoyed routine experiences, like reading a magazine and
talking with a friend.

The psychologists found, as you might guess, that the lottery winners
highly appreciated winning the lottery and the accident victims felt sad-
dened by their traumatic injuries. Now, here is what is remarkable. When
comparing the lottery winners to the randomly selected control group, the
researchers found *no differences* in happiness either at the time of the inter-
views (present happiness) or in their levels of expected future happiness.
The lottery winners were not happier than the non–lottery winners after

the initial happiness associated with winning the lottery had passed. Most interestingly, the winners experienced significantly *less* pleasure in daily activities than did the members of the other two groups.

My intention is not to start this book off on a somber note, but to consider whether we really know what will bring us joy. We may think, "If I only had this sports car, a place in Maui, or cheesecake, I will have won the emotional lottery!" Yet research—and, if we pause to examine it, our own experience—show otherwise. Timothy Wilson and Daniel Gilbert (2005, 131) explain, "People routinely mispredict how much pleasure or displeasure future events will bring, and as a result, sometimes work to bring about events that do not maximize their happiness." How do we know what to want? We often make decisions based on *affective forecasts*, or predictions of how we will feel in the future (Wilson and Gilbert 2005). Yet people are generally not great at predicting the intensity of future emotional reactions. We may be wrong about how positive or negative our responses will be in actuality.

Not only do we often mispredict how much pleasure we will experience, we also often overestimate how much pain we will endure. Do you ever think, "I won't survive this," and actually cope better than you had anticipated? Decisions about how to cope with difficult emotions, and ideas about how much pleasure we may derive from eating, may be based on predictions about our future feelings. And those forecasts are likely inaccurate. In the pages to come, we will work to revisit some of our beliefs about the downside of feeling and the upside of eating, learning to hold these ideas and beliefs lightly and compassionately, without judgment or fear, seeing them for what they are.

What Is Emotional Eating?

Most of us have a general, rational sense of what to eat and when—there is no shortage of information on the subject. Yet there is often a disconnect between what we know and what we do. We may have the facts, but decisions also involve our feelings. Many people who struggle with difficult emotions also struggle with eating problems. *Emotional eating* is a popular term used to describe eating that is influenced by emotions, both positive and negative. Feelings may affect various aspects of your eating, including your motivation to eat, your food choices, where and with whom you eat, and the speed at which you eat. Most overeating is prompted by feelings rather than physical hunger. Individuals who struggle with obesity tend to eat in response to emotions (Ganley 1989). However, people who eat for emotional reasons are not necessarily overweight. People of any size may try to escape an emotional experience by preoccupying themselves with eating or by obsessing over their shape and weight.

Here are some examples of what emotional eating may look like:

- Snacking when you do not feel physically hungry or when you are moderately full

- Experiencing an intense craving for a particular food

- Not feeling satiated after eating adequate amounts of healthy food

- Anxiously gathering more food while your mouth is full

- Feeling emotionally relieved while eating

- Eating during or following a stressful experience

- Numbing feelings with food

- Eating alone to avoid others noticing

People who eat for emotional reasons often eat in an attempt to self-soothe or to experience momentary relief from difficult feelings. Some people describe purposely eating certain comforting foods as a way to cope with stress. Emotional eating is related to feelings of inadequacy (Waller and Osman 1998). Emotions may seem so intense that we feel we need to instantly manage them by escaping with food, or we may feel we lack other tools to cope with distress.

Think about your own experience. Do you experience authentic or lasting relief while eating? Or is relief fleeting or partial at best? Just as when we compulsively watch television, drink alcohol, or shop, we may wish to temporarily escape through eating. In later chapters, I will introduce some more skillful means to cope with distress. In this chapter, you will learn how to better understand emotions so that you will feel less averse to or overwhelmed by your feelings.

Understanding Eating Disorders

Emotional eating is not in itself a specific eating disorder, though emotional eating occurs in eating disorders. Emotional eating is associated with binge eating, obesity, and bulimia (e.g., Lindeman and Stark 2001). You may or may not have an eating disorder, but from time to time I will mention eating disorders to illustrate the ways emotions affect eating disorder behaviors. First, I'll briefly clarify how the *Diagnostic and Statistical Manual of Mental Disorders—Fourth Edition (DSM-IV-TR)* categorizes eating disorders.

Anorexia involves overevaluation of shape and weight. People who struggle with anorexia define their self-worth largely based on their weight. In this disorder, individuals maintain an abnormally low body weight (less than 85 percent of normal). To meet criteria for anorexia, a woman must lose her menstrual period as a result of her dietary restriction.

Bulimia similarly includes overevaluation of one's shape and weight and rigid efforts to control one's body. People who struggle with bulimia recurrently binge, or consume an objectively large amount of food, and experience a loss of control while doing so. In addition to bingeing, people with bulimia engage in certain compensatory behaviors, or attempts to "make up" for excessive caloric intake, by restricting food intake, vomiting, overexercising, or misusing laxatives.

Eating disorder not otherwise specified (NOS) is the most common eating disorder. This category describes an eating disorder of clinical severity that does not meet criteria for anorexia or bulimia. For example, a woman who is a healthy weight but finds herself excessively preoccupied with concerns about her shape may meet criteria for eating disorder NOS. A man who is preoccupied with his shape and restricts his food intake but does not weigh less than 85 percent of normal would similarly receive the eating disorder NOS diagnosis.

One form of eating disorder NOS is binge-eating disorder. Binge-eating disorder describes recurrent binge eating in the absence of extreme efforts to control weight, and this disorder often correlates with obesity—though it can also occur in people who are normal weight. Unlike anorexia or bulimia, which overwhelmingly affect women and girls, approximately a third of people who binge eat are male.

Let's take a moment to differentiate objective binges from subjective binges. An *objective binge* describes consuming an objectively large amount of food, accompanied by a sense of loss of control. A person may consume thousands of calories in a sitting in an objective binge. A *subjective binge* involves feeling or thinking you ate too much. If you overindulge on Thanksgiving, this would be a subjective binge if you ate what is normal in that context but you still feel like you overate. Distinguishing objective binges from subjective ones can help us begin to move away from seeing our behaviors in absolute terms or engaging in black-and-white thinking about those behaviors. Feeling or thinking you ate too much differs from losing control and rapidly consuming excessive calories.

Most eating disorders share certain core features, and many people who meet the criteria for one eating disorder end up meeting the criteria for another eating disorder at some point (Fairburn 2008). For example, someone who struggles with anorexia may eventually receive a diagnosis of bulimia. Generally, people who struggle with eating disorders overevaluate their shape and weight and are intensely preoccupied in attempts to manage their size. Binge eating is also very common across eating disorders. Conceptually, this makes sense. If you define yourself by your weight, you may restrict your food, and restricting food often results in overeating, as you start to feel deprived. After a diet people may tend to indulge in foods they craved during the diet. People often also binge in response to negative moods or to having a difficult day.

Eating and Emotions

People may either increase or decrease their eating as a result of distress. For example, some people experience an increase in appetite when they feel depressed, while others experience a decrease. Restricting food may be a way to manage emotions, as may bingeing. You may find yourself indulging when you feel difficult emotions in order to soothe yourself, and then putting yourself on harsh diets in an attempt to control your weight and your feelings.

Psychologists theorize that difficulty in managing emotions is the core issue underlying both binge eating and bulimia. Binge eating and other forms of problematic eating are often seen as behavioral attempts to influence, change, or control painful emotional states (Safer, Telch, and Chen 2009; Linehan and Chen 2005). People who don't know how to manage emotions, either positive or negative, may resort to binge eating and/or purging as a way to manage emotions. Anorexia is similarly driven by attempts to avoid emotion (e.g., Wildes, Ringham, and Marcus 2010). Specifically, reduced awareness of emotions can occur in people with bulimia, and emotional avoidance is characteristic of those who struggle with anorexia (Legenbauer, Vocks, and Rüddel 2008; Wildes, Ringham, and Marcus 2010).

Emotions may affect eating in more subtle ways that do not register clinically. For example, how many of us have dived into a tray of cupcakes after a breakup? There is nothing wrong with enjoying food during a rough time, but regularly depending on food to manage our feelings sends us the unhelpful message "You can't cope." Plus, what does a cupcake do to honor your feelings or to clarify what matters to you?

Research finds that difficulty in identifying and understanding emotions, as well as problems in regulating them, influences binge eating more than gender, food restriction, or overvaluing shape and weight do (Whiteside et al. 2007). When people experience emotions intensely, or have trouble identifying what their emotions actually are, they may feel that they cannot cope with their feelings and may then try to avoid the discomfort by distracting themselves with food.

You may notice that you simply jump from feeling any intense emotion to eating, thus losing contact with the emotion. This may feel like a relief at first, but it results in your missing the opportunity to experience the feeling for what it is (this is something you can practice doing, as we will see). It is inevitable that we will experience uncomfortable feelings, and consistently avoiding them limits our ability to live both freely and wisely. Certain people are more *emotionally vulnerable*, experiencing emotions more intensely and feeling emotions for a longer time than others (Linehan 1993a). If you are emotionally vulnerable and were raised in an environment where you were not taught how to cope with feelings—or worse, were punished for showing emotions—you may have learned to control feelings with food.

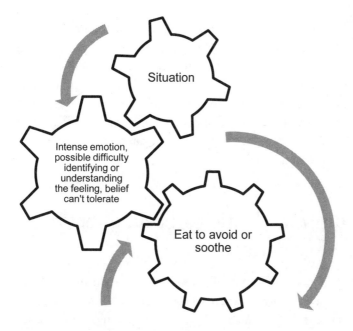

Figure 1: Cycle of Emotional Eating

When you experience an emotion and eat in response, you may experience more of the same emotion, as well as other emotions that arise in response to emotional eating. Eating to turn off feelings doesn't fully appease your feelings; instead it just adds more psychological (and caloric) weight to the experience. Also, if you eat in response to feelings, you often fail to appreciate the message the feelings relay. Notably, anger and sadness are especially related to problematic eating (e.g., Fox and Froom 2009); many people also notice they tend to eat when happy, lonely, or anxious. Eating Southern fried chicken may initially seem soothing, but overindulging in comfort foods at a time when your emotions are powerful can dampen valuable emotional information, as well as eventually lead to shame and confusion.

Food may also be used to increase the intensity of an emotion. We may, for example, use food to add to the ordinary experience of happiness, attempting to take our joy up a notch. Gracie, a former client of mine, struggled with an intense depression for a year. After a combination of cognitive behavioral therapy and medication, her mood improved and she began to relish food. She described eating as relearning pleasure. Initially, Gracie loved exploring new wines and cheeses. Eventually, she guzzled wines and gobbled cheeses in search of an endless celestial taste experience. Gracie had gone too far. The simple joy of eating was replaced by a manic insatiability. The short-term benefits of becoming a cheese maven and unofficial sommelier were now being negated by anxiety and shame around her increasing weight.

Exercise: Noticing Feelings before and after Eating

Grab your notebook and call to mind a situation in which you recently overate or ate when you weren't especially hungry. As nonjudgmentally as you can, answer the following questions. You are simply gathering information here; if difficult feelings come up while you are doing the exercise, try to notice them and gently return your attention to the question.

1. What was the situation (where were you, whom were you with, what was happening, what was about to happen, or what had just happened)?

2. As best you can, consider, now that you have some distance, what emotions were present. What were you feeling?

3. How did the emotions affect your eating (for example, did you eat more than you intended, or more quickly, or choose a food you may not typically eat)?

4. Now bring to mind the emotions you experienced after eating. What were they?

When you mindfully notice the feelings that prompt eating, you practice bringing your awareness, not your guilt, to your habits. You can do this exercise again and again, always as compassionately and nonjudgmentally as you can; the practice of noticing will give you a helpful perspective on how your emotions and your eating intersect. In a moment of emotional distress, it may be difficult to hold on to that perspective, but over time you will become more able to say, for example, "Ah, there is loneliness, and there is that familiar pull to eat." You will begin to have a choice about how to handle the loneliness.

♥

Why Do We Have Emotions?

Let's step back for a moment and consider the functions in feelings. Emotions furnish us with valuable information. The root of the word "emotion" is *motere*, from the Latin for "to move." Emotions quickly generate changes in our brain and spinal cord to initiate action—our behavior is often closely tied to emotion. An emotion is a *brief* signal promoting survival behavior. *Emotions motivate our behavior, provide us with valuable information, and allow us to communicate with others* (Linehan 1993b).

Let's consider two common emotions and their functions. Say your partner befriends a remarkably attractive colleague, and you experience jealousy. Why? Because an emotion (jealousy) signals a threat, inspiring us to formulate behaviors in response to that threat. When we feel jealous, we are provided with information that our relationship is precious and may be in danger. Jealous behavior communicates our uneasiness to our partner; thus jealousy directs us toward protecting the relationship. If we eat to suppress this emotion or to distract ourselves from it, we can't learn what the emotion is telling us, and we can't react in an appropriate way, such as expressing our feelings to our partner. Similarly, what is the value in feeling happy? Happiness motivates us to continue pursuing an activity or valued direction. The feeling provides information on what matters to us. Happiness also communicates information to those around us, cementing vital social bonds. Would a friend be as inclined to invite you to a birthday dinner if you looked miserable at the previous event she hosted?

Mario's Story

When Mario came to me for therapy, he explained that he worried about everything. He was newly married and in the midst of purchasing an expensive home that would require investing his life savings, barely leaving money for the necessary renovations. "Did I marry the right person? Am I going crazy? Is my mind working? I seem forgetful. What if the plane I take to Miami crashes? Will my father develop Parkinson's like my grandfather?" The worries were endless, and Mario noticed that the more he worried the more he felt depressed. To ease his tortured mind, he spent time distracting himself by eating.

Over the course of cognitive behavioral therapy with an emphasis on mindfulness and acceptance, Mario began to learn to not panic over his feelings of panic. He became able to bring awareness to his worries as mental processes rather than get stuck in his mind, where he would live in the worst-case scenarios. He practiced asking himself, "Is this worry productive or unproductive?" If a worry was productive, he came up with an action plan. If it was unproductive, he noticed the feelings and thoughts in his body and mind and practiced returning to the present moment. When he noticed urges to reach for sweets and salty foods as he tensed up, he chose to sit with his feelings instead, seeing his feelings as meaningful.

What sat behind his worries? He deeply valued serving as a provider, establishing a secure, loving home, and protecting his father. His feelings reflected what mattered to him, though his relationship with his feelings—profound fear and confusion about feeling too much and not understanding his feelings—got in the way of his willingness to accept and learn from his emotions. During our last session, he said, "I feel because things matter to me. I can talk to my wife about our difficulties, take action to solve financial problems, and show my dad how much I care. That tastes sweet in my heart."

Exercise: Considering the Functions of Difficult Feelings

Take a few moments to recreate the following chart in your notebook. The point of this exercise is to practice considering, like Mario, how your feelings provide meaningful information. Given that negative emotions feel uncomfortable, it makes a lot of sense that you may try to escape feeling them. By understanding the functions of emotions, you may change your responses to your emotions. This example shows how Mario might have used the chart to discover his feelings, their value, and the actions he might take based on them.

Situation	Emotion(s)	What does this emotion communicate to me?	What does this emotion communicate to others?	What action(s) does this emotion motivate me to take?	Is this action (or actions) helpful?
Mario gets an unexpected bill	1. Anxiety	1. I have many financial responsibilities, and it's important to me that I meet them.	When I am anxious and ashamed it is hard for me to talk to my wife. I've told her that when I feel this way, it's hard to open up and she reaches out to me.	1. Figure out how to start saving more, and do it	1. Yes
	2. Shame about lack of money in savings	2. I believe that as the man of the family I should be better prepared financially than I am.		2. Eat to soothe myself	2. No

Beliefs about Emotions

We all have beliefs about emotions—for example, you might believe that it is weak to feel sad or that it is weak to feel sad or afraid. Common beliefs about emotions include:

- Negative emotions are bad.

- If I feel too happy, I may lose control.

- I don't deserve to experience positive emotions.

- If I feel happy, I should take it up a notch.

- I need to control difficult feelings because otherwise I'll feel too much.

- It is depressing to feel sad—I may not be able to pull out of it if I let myself feel it.

- I may get sick from worrying.

- If I try harder, I can get rid of a feeling.

- No one else feels the way I do.

- If I hide my feelings, no one will know how I feel and I may stop feeling this way.

- Distracting myself from an emotion is better than feeling it.

- I'll never be able to figure out how I feel; there are too many feelings happening.

- I'm not feeling the way I *should* feel.

What we believe about emotions affects how we feel and how we behave when an emotion arises. Plus, remember that our hypotheses about how we will feel in the future are often inaccurate. Emotions may feel overwhelming when we assume that they will last forever or when we believe that we cannot cope with them, but is that really the case? People who label emotions as bad or unhealthy may try to escape emotions by binge eating (Leahy 2002). Take a moment to reflect: What are your beliefs about emotions—either in general, or for particular emotions? What are your beliefs about your ability to manage emotions? How do these beliefs affect your behavior? Given what you now know about the function of emotions, are your beliefs helpful—that is, do they lead to helpful behaviors? The following exercise will help you answer these questions.

Exercise: Thinking about Feeling

Often, our beliefs are long held and so deeply rooted that the behaviors they trigger in us feel automatic. By bringing our awareness to what we believe about emotions, we can give ourselves more room to choose how we respond to the feelings when they arise. Reproduce the following chart in your notebook, filling in the lines for any emotion you have noticeable beliefs about. An example follows.

	My beliefs about this emotion	How these beliefs affect me	Is this helpful?	Alternative ways I could think about this emotion
Joy				
Sadness				
Fear				
Anger				
Shame				
Other emotion				

	My beliefs about this emotion	How these beliefs affect me	Is this helpful?	Alternative ways I could think about this emotion
Joy	I don't deserve to be happy.	I feel guilty when I experience happiness or enjoy myself.	No; my feeling guilty doesn't help anyone.	Everyone deserves to be happy, including me. I'm kinder to others when I'm happy.
Sadness	When I feel sad, it lasts for weeks.	I worry a lot about being sad or giving in to sadness.	No; the worry doesn't make the sadness disappear—it makes it worse.	Emotions come and go. I have always recovered from sadness before, sometimes in a short time.
Other emotion (Love)	If I feel love, I may get hurt.	I avoid dating.	No; the loneliness hurts, too.	It is true I might get hurt or suffer loss in love, but I can cope with difficult emotions. Loving and being loved, and sometimes getting hurt, is part of being alive.

The Freedom in Noticing and Labeling Feelings

When we *sit with our emotions*—that is, when we allow ourselves to experience them—one of the first steps is to accurately identify and label the emotion (e.g., Linehan 1993b). *When we can accurately label an emotion, we're observing it without judgment.* In noticing an emotion without judgment, we are also accepting it. What is the benefit in noticing that we feel "anxious" rather than identifying this emotion as just "feeling bad?" We become separate from an emotion when we give it a name; we're not judging it as "good" or "bad"—it just is what it is, and it does not define us. This helps us avoid being emotionally hijacked by it—labeling ourselves either "good" or "bad" along with the emotion. Labeling an emotion also provides us with information on how to cope with it. If you can label your emotion, and differentiate among your emotions, you can manage them flexibly (Feldman Barrett et al. 2001). When you replace "I'm feeling bad" with "I'm feeling anxious and experiencing shame," you have more specific information on how to deal with the feeling. To use a medical analogy, treatment for a sinus infection is different from treatment for the stomach flu. Similarly, the way you navigate loneliness differs from the way you would manage anger—not least because emotions convey important information, and the message of loneliness is very different from the message of anger.

Thoughts may affect how we feel, and feelings may affect how we think. We'll talk in more detail about noticing our thoughts in chapter 6. But briefly, it may be helpful to begin to notice how thoughts and feelings may influence one another. A given situation may trigger a particular thought, which then sparks a certain feeling; or it may happen the other way around, with the situation engendering a feeling that then leads to a thought. For example, we may find ourselves standing in front of a large crowd before we present a speech. We may begin to think, "I can't do this," and then experience a feeling of panic. Or we may simply begin to feel panic, and then think, "I can't do this." Can you think of a situation where your feelings influenced your thinking, and another where your thinking affected your feelings? (I'll address how to modify and manage thoughts and feelings in the chapters ahead.)

Certain emotions are actually combinations of feelings and thoughts. "Hopelessness," for example, is sadness combined with a belief that the situation will not improve. Can you think of another feeling that also includes a thought?

Some people find it challenging to label emotions. If you find that's the case for you, it can help to familiarize yourself with categories of emotions; with situations that may lead to certain feelings; with the adaptive functions of emotions (that is, the ways an emotion aids in our survival); and with how you may think, feel, and behave when you experience them. Here are some common emotional categories.

Fear

Function: to protect us from immediate danger

Synonyms: fright, panic, uneasiness, terror

Typical prompting events: facing a threat; performing before others; facing a new situation

Typical accompanying thoughts: "I can't handle this"; "I'm going to fail"; "I'm in danger."

Common body sensations: racing heart, unsettled stomach, nausea, lump in the throat, breathlessness, jumpiness

Common actions related to fear: running, freezing up, screaming, crying, seeking safety

Anxiety

Function: to protect us from future danger

Synonyms: nervousness, worry, stress, overwhelm

Typical prompting event: thinking about or imagining a future feared situation

Typical accompanying thoughts: "I won't be able to handle this"; "He'll leave me"; "What if...?"

Common body sensations: difficulty relaxing, tension and muscle tightness, sleeplessness, difficulty concentrating, racing heart, queasy stomach, jitteriness

Common actions related to anxiety: avoiding people or places that engender fear; seeking reassurance from others

Anger

Function: to allow us to respond to a violation

Synonyms: annoyed, irritated, upset, offended

Typical prompting events: feeling threatened; not getting what you want; experiencing physical or emotional pain

Typical accompanying thoughts: "I don't deserve this"; "I will not tolerate this"; "It's not fair."

Common body sensations: body and facial tension, flushed face, clenching fists, tightness in jaw

Common actions related to anger: defending, threatening, yelling, withdrawing

Sadness

Function: to slow us down, allowing us to cope with the loss of a person or desired goal

Synonyms: unhappiness, hurt, misery, sorrow

Typical prompting events: experiencing loss or rejection; feeling powerless

Typical associated thoughts: "This is a big loss"; "There's no hope."

Common body sensations: loss of energy, urge to cry, heaviness in the stomach, difficulty concentrating

Common actions related to sadness: lying in bed, self-isolating, losing motivation or interest

Joy

Function: to prompt us to celebrate something we value

Synonyms: happiness, excitement, delight, enjoyment, gladness

Typical prompting events: feeling successful; receiving love or praise

Typical accompanying thoughts: "This is wonderful"; "I'm so lucky."

Common body sensations: smiling, relaxed body, feeling energized

Common actions related to joy: continuing activities engendering joy, celebrating, acting silly

Shame

Function: to prompt us to correct behavior that violates social norms

Synonyms: embarrassment, remorse

Prompting event: disobeying a rule in your community

Typical accompanying thought: "I hope no one finds out."

Typical body sensations: blushing, racing heart

Typical actions related to shame: hiding, attempting to repair the damage

Guilt

Function: to permit us to live according to our personal values

Synonyms: remorse, responsibility

Typical prompting event: doing something you believe is wrong

Typical accompanying thought: "I did something bad."

Common body sensations: queasy stomach, difficulty relaxing, muscle tension

Common actions related to guilt: apologizing, reflecting, changing behavior

Disgust

Function: to prompt us to move away from something or someone contaminating

Synonyms: revulsion, aversion

Typical prompting event: facing something harmful

Typical accompanying thoughts: "This will make me sick"; "I need to get away."

Common body sensations: nausea, uneasiness

Common actions related to disgust: pushing away, avoiding, expressing concern

Interest

Function: to alert us to potential rewards

Synonyms: excitement, curiosity

Typical prompting event: participating in an experience that grabs your attention

Typical accompanying thoughts: "This may be great"; "How can I get involved?"

Common body sensations: widened eyes

Common actions related to interest: moving toward, getting more information

Exercise: SIFTing through Emotions

Emotions create links between a situation, our interpretations of it, feelings in our bodies, and tendencies to act. To practice familiarizing yourself with your feelings, try to slow down in a situation where emotions are arising and bring your awareness to how you feel. Use the acronym SIFT (Situation, Interpretations, Feelings, Tendencies) to work through the factors that affect your experience of emotions. If it's helpful, grab your notebook and use the following questions to examine the feelings you experienced in a recent highly emotional situation.

First, notice what **emotions** you are having. Note the intensity of your emotion on a scale from 1 (barely there) to 10 (extreme). Now SIFT your emotions:

S: What is the **situation** (the event or person that triggered an emotional reaction)?

I: Do you notice **interpretations** or thoughts that relate to your experience?

F: What **feelings** and sensations do you notice in your body?

T: What **tendencies** show up? Are you pulled to pursue particular actions?

♥

Labeling an emotion (even one that is not your own) helps you regulate your emotions. When you label an emotion, you treat emotions as *objects* of attention, promoting a certain amount of distance. In a study at the University of California, Los Angeles, David Creswell and his colleagues (2007) showed participants photographs of emotionally expressive faces and instructed them to either label the emotion (e.g., sad) or choose a gender-appropriate name (e.g., Bob or Sue) for the person in the photo. Participants' brain activity was recorded using functional magnetic resonance imaging (fMRI). The alarm center of the brain was less active when an emotion label was attached, compared to a name label.

Noticing All Feelings

At times, certain emotions can feel so intense that they overshadow others. Doug Mennin and David Fresco (2009), experts in the area of emotion regulation in anxiety disorders, describe this experience as trying to listen as a cacophonous tuba drowns the pitch of a modest flute. As we contemplate flying to visit a family member, for example, we may feel afraid to the point that we lose contact with our subtler feeling of joy. Or we may feel immersed in self-hate to the degree that we fail to notice other emotions and their messages. Like the tuba, a tub of gelato—and the emotional consequences of indulging in it—may distance us from the full range of our emotions.

Do you notice a particular emotion that often drowns out other feelings that may be present? For example, does fear obscure your experience of excitement? Does sadness rapidly melt into anger? When an emotion feels incredibly intense and impossible to regulate, it may be helpful to practice distress tolerance, which we will discuss in chapter 7. Meanwhile, use the following exercise to map out the full range of emotions you experience within a particular situation, including their relative intensity.

Exercise: Noticing All Feelings

When you overeat, are there particular emotions that seem so powerful that you can feel nothing else? For this exercise, compassionately consider a situation where an emotion felt very intense, and you turned to eating in response. Did other feelings whisper alongside the strong emotion or emotions? In your notebook, write answers to the following questions, practicing bringing your awareness to all emotions you experienced in this situation.

First, notice what **emotions** you are having. Note the intensity of your emotion on a scale from 1 (barely there) to 10 (extreme). Now SIFT your emotions, as in the earlier exercise:

S: What was the **situation** (event or encounter) that led to emotion?

I: What **interpretations** or thoughts did you notice that relate to your experience?

F: What **feelings** and sensations do you notice in your body?

T: What **tendencies** show up? Are you pulled to pursue particular actions?

♥

When an emotion gets you stuck, overshadows other emotions and experiences, and pulls you away from the moment and what matters to you, it is skillful to be able to notice and label this process and return to the present. Consider: is there an emotion you struggle with that frequently moves you away from what matters to you? If so, and you can identify it, just sit with it gently for the time being. I'll address accessing the present moment more thoroughly in chapter 3 and clarifying what you value in chapter 9.

Summary

As Robert Frost simply stated, "The only way out is through." In this chapter, you began learning to systematically and nonjudgmentally notice your thoughts and beliefs about emotions and the ways those thoughts, beliefs, and emotions can link up with behaviors. You learned that, for many people, emotions may seem too difficult to bear or to understand and that this can lead to eating to soothe and escape (among other compulsive self-soothing behaviors). Learning to appreciate the functions of feelings, explore your beliefs about feelings, and notice and label feelings are the first steps in breaking the chain linking your feelings with food.

Chapter 2

ACCEPTING THE IDEA
OF ACCEPTANCE

The curious paradox is that when I accept myself just as I
am, then I can change.

—CARL ROGERS

What is truly behind emotional eating? It is our unwillingness to accept, or sit with, our emotions. But when we eat for emotional reasons, we don't ever actually rid ourselves of our emotions. Rather, entering into and accepting our emotions is the doorway to freedom and joy, as well as relief from the cycle of emotional eating. But this can be hard to hear. Even my most gracious clients shudder when I say the word "accept" in the context of emotions and eating. Who wants to accept difficult feelings or pain, or accept a weight that feels unacceptable? It can feel like I'm advising giving up. I humbly suggest that this very process, a soulful new paradigm, is the key to a new and kinder relationship with food. Diets, food plans, mixing and matching, supplementing, and depriving may temporarily help. Accepting, moment to moment, is a long-term solution. Far from being painful, acceptance is a form of kindness: you acknowledge your truths and where you are in this moment of your life. Will your weight go down as your mind expands? Maybe. Will your suffering decrease? Yes. As you will read in this book, acceptance will not preclude change; rather, acceptance accompanies change. Fighting your body brings stagnation. Acceptance brings flow.

Understanding Acceptance

Have you ever eaten to cope with feeling fat? Too often, people want to lose weight yesterday and get frustrated when their weight-loss attempts seem to go slowly. The process of weight loss has become more like a disease treatment than an adventure to pursue. One might argue that obesity is a serious health problem, or eating for emotional reasons rather than hunger cues is problematic. At the same time, would we encourage a person with depression to achieve better mental health by dwelling on how low his mood is, or would we encourage him to accept his mood—not in the spirit of despairing of ever improving, but of creatively and enthusiastically seeking original solutions? The nature of this ongoing journey requires constantly returning to an acceptance of self and of setbacks and new challenges.

The origin of the word "accept" is the Latin for "to take." This is fitting because, paradoxically, *the only way to reduce suffering is by taking pain.* The basic equations are:

Pain = Pain

Pain + Nonacceptance = Suffering

Acceptance is *not* resignation. It does not necessarily include liking or condoning pain. But if the word "acceptance" is making you itch, you may replace it with a term like "expansiveness." Acceptance is purposely adopting an open, nonjudgmental, receptive stance, even when faced with challenge. This includes accepting our emotions, thoughts, sensations, body shape, and reality in general, just as it is in this moment. Nonacceptance—fighting reality or our emotions—limits our awareness and extends our struggle. Imagine holding onto one end of a scarf as I hold onto the other end. If the scarf symbolizes your weight, what is your relationship with it? Are we relaxed as we hold the scarf together, or is there tension—are we pulling in opposite directions? For a moment, consider the physical and emotional experience involved in a tug-of-war. It monopolizes our attention and energy. Is it worth it? What is the alternative? We could let go of the fight, dropping the pull and freeing up our hands and energy.

If we are willing to participate only in situations that feel good, what is our life about? When we are unwilling to accept our reality, we drastically narrow our options. That being said, we can determine *how* to meet and accept situations. Acceptance, in the sense I am using the term, is about compassion and self-respect, not masochism. It is complex and dynamic—an ongoing series of choices that relate our thoughts and actions to our deep values. *Values* describe what deeply matters to you or what you want your life to stand for (we'll address values in detail in chapter 9). You may choose to accept engaging in a challenging relationship with a loved one if doing so relates to your value of supporting your loved ones ("I will visit Mom at Christmas and help her clear out the attic"), while also doing what you need to do to in the service of your value of protecting and caring for yourself ("I'll stay at a hotel so I have my own place to go to if things start getting rough"). If you are able to accept the realities of a situation, rather than hoping or fantasizing things will somehow be different this time, you can take actions that honor both sets of values. Similarly, you may accept both your current shape and the emotional and behavioral commitments required to change it. You may accept your feelings and simultaneously change the way you respond to them (Linehan 1993a). You do not have to accept constant hunger and self-torture.

Often, when we experience pain, we find ourselves angry with others, blaming ourselves, or reacting impulsively. I recently found myself waiting in the service line at my mobile phone service provider. I noticed a woman next to me telling a story about how the company had wasted her time and requesting a free iPhone case to compensate her. She told the story repeatedly—to the salesperson, assistant manager, and manager. I noticed she became more tense, loud, and exasperated—and lost more time—with each repetition. Eventually, she began to threaten canceling her phone service, which I could foresee would create even greater agitation for her. I felt my heart soften both for her and for the employees who were dealing with her, who experienced pain in the encounter. She was stuck on proving her point rather than accepting certain facts, and in the process, she experienced more pain and lost time and also caused others distress.

When we are ambushed by our emotions, it can be a challenge to slow down and notice whether our feelings are based in reality and whether our actions are serving our well-being and our values.

Acceptance entails recognizing reality as it is, nonjudgmentally understanding the causes of this reality, and engaging with it rather than fighting against it (Linehan 1993b). Acceptance means pursuing effective behaviors rather than getting stuck in judgments regarding what is "right" or "wrong," "fair" or "unfair."

Radical Acceptance

Acceptance is an *active* process entailing being open to the experience of what is, as it is, at *each* moment. "Acceptance without commitment is a shallow victory, and commitment is not sustainable without acceptance" (Zettle 2007, 13). Acceptance is psychological as well as behavioral, involving accepting with both our mind and our actions. Accepting our reality entirely—the only really effective form of acceptance—is called *radical acceptance* (Linehan 1993b). It is difficult to accept what is in the moment entirely; however, only partially accepting our reality will not help our suffering. Imagine that you "accept" your mother-in-law, though when you see her you incessantly think about how awful she is as a person. What does this sort of acceptance accomplish? You may intellectually accept her, but you still feel tense and stressed when she's around, and you can barely stand to speak to her. If you radically accept your current weight or shape, you are neither grimacing when you look in the mirror nor resigning yourself to doing nothing about it.

Acceptance means noticing without judgment. This does not mean you are not allowed to have a thought like "I can't stand the way I look"—it just means you are able to notice it when you have it ("that's a thought"). This labeling can allow you to simply have and notice the thought without having to attach despair or shame to it. You don't suppress the thought, and you don't dwell on it—you watch it come and you watch it go. In this case, you've had a judgment, but you didn't judge the judgment—you just noticed it—and this dulls its sting and may also allow you to look at the content of the judging thought. As you might imagine, this is a practice that no one ever gets perfectly—we are all human—but once you begin doing it, it's always there and available for you to use as you are able. (We'll talk about this process more later in this chapter.)

Imagine yourself, again, in front of the mirror. Acceptance also involves approaching the situation with both a literal and a figurative posture of willingness—perhaps literally relaxing your neck and shoulders, smoothing your forehead, and unfolding your arms as you look in the mirror. This can help you notice the thought "I can't stand the way I look" without buying into it. There is a feedback loop between our physical posture and our brain; again, in order to move toward acceptance, it is important to do so with both mind and body. If your mind accepts something while your body tenses, signaling rejection, are you radically accepting your reality? The following exercise will give you practice in noticing the relationship between your body and your mind when it comes to acceptance.

Exercise: Practicing Radical Acceptance

You may either think about or write about a distressing fact in your life. Don't feel obligated to select the most challenging. Instead, choose something that seems difficult yet possible to accept.

1. What is the situation? Just think about or write down the facts, noticing them without judgment or opinion.

2. Practice tensing your body as you think about this situation. Try raising your hands so your forearms are at 90-degree angles to your upper arms and clench your fists and facial muscles by raising your eyebrows and pursing your lips. What do you notice about how you feel about the situation?

3. Now practice letting go of the tension while thinking about the situation, opening your hands, releasing tension in your forehead, and relaxing your body as you sit with the reality of the situation. Relax your face, slightly turning up the corners

of your mouth. Sit for several minutes like this. What do you notice about your emotions around this situation?

Example:

1. I weigh fifty pounds more than I would like. I've steadily been gaining about two pounds a month over the last two years. It's hard for me to lose weight without changing my eating.

2. As I tense my body, I feel even heavier and more uncomfortable. The fifty pounds seems to weigh more in my mind and body.

3. As I release, I feel like I'm beginning to move forward. I look at this fact more openly. I feel less heavy and more ready to commit to a plan.

♥

Returning When the Mind Has Moved away from Acceptance

When you move toward acceptance, you don't land at once at your destination. Rather, you may accept a situation, notice that the urge to fight reality arises, and turn again toward the recognition of reality, over and over again (Linehan 1993b). Part of practicing acceptance is accepting the process itself. When you notice that you are not accepting, that is a moment of awareness and an opportunity to begin again in the practice of acceptance. You can accept your nonacceptance as well. Use the following exercise to practice returning to acceptance.

Exercise: Practicing Returning to Acceptance

This exercise is intended to help you notice nonacceptance and practice returning from nonacceptance to acceptance.

1. Choose a food that you really enjoy, and make the decision to practice portion control for this food during a single meal. Put a normal-sized serving of the food on your plate.

2. Before you begin, pause a moment to fully accept the process of sticking to this serving size and accepting any discomfort that may visit.

3. Eat slowly enough that you have time to notice the thoughts, feelings, and sensations that arise. Finish the serving and do not serve yourself more. You may notice judgmental thoughts, such as "I can't control myself." You may notice tension in your body, or your mouth watering as you put down your fork after the last bite. Accepting entails noticing it all and not fighting, whether by choosing to exceed your intended portion or by suffering as you move away.

4. Write down the thoughts and emotions you had as you accepted that you wanted more while deciding not to indulge, or as you allowed yourself to eat all of a normal-sized portion.

5. Notice what it feels like if you move away from acceptance; is there tension in your mind or body?

6. Can you turn again toward acceptance when you find yourself moving away? You may find yourself doing it repeatedly. Write about how this process felt for you.

♥

Willingness vs. Willfulness

Acceptance includes having an attitude of willingness, or openness, around choosing to accept what is, rather than fighting, evading, or attempting to control reality. If we are willing to experience the feelings and sensations that come with what's happening, we can then accept them. Without willingness, we aren't truly accepting our situation. Willingness is akin to wonder and has a proactive quality. Willfulness—the intent to have our own way—resembles intolerance and passivity. Gerald May (1982, 6) defines willingness as:

a realization that one already is a part of some ultimate cosmic process and...a commitment to participation in that process. In contrast, willfulness is the setting of oneself apart from the fundamental essence of life in an attempt to master, direct, control, or otherwise manipulate existence. More simply, willingness is saying yes to the mystery of being alive in each moment. Willfulness is saying no, or perhaps more commonly, "Yes, but..."

For example, if you embodied willingness as a novice dancer in an advanced dance class, you would continue to participate with enthusiasm—even if you made mistakes—rather than standing on the side or leaving the class when it started to get challenging. You would not get stuck in your mind in comparisons between your poise and that of a former principal dancer in the New York City Ballet. Leaving the class or getting stuck in your mind is willfulness, the stance of rejecting reality. How often have you said, "I will try"? If you stood on the outskirts of this dance class (or your life), what would "trying" look like? The choice is really between doing and not doing (Eifert and Forsyth 2005).

Willingness is persistently practicing acceptance regardless of the outcome. You don't have to *feel* willing to *behave* willingly. If you are driving behind a person moving twenty miles below the speed limit and cannot change lanes, willing actions include relaxing your face and body, driving slowly, suspending judgment as best you can, and staying alert to an opportunity to change lanes safely. Unwilling actions include cursing, slamming on your horn, and tailgating.

Acceptance entails a willingness to experience whatever thoughts, emotions, and sensations arise, rather than avoiding them. Willingness is making the compassionate choice to participate in the moment. The alternative—fighting reality—reinforces a sense that you cannot cope, which is neither compassionate nor empowering. And unwillingness to experience an emotion, rather than the emotion itself, often leads us to eat comfort foods (Evers, Stok, and De Ridder 2010).

You may wish to end emotional eating, lose weight, or rid yourself of difficult emotions, but are you willing to actively accept what is in this moment and in each step of the process? Willfulness is similar to wishing your problems away; willingness is accepting what is and actively participating in the process of change. Remember, though, willingness is a practice, not a state of being; no one is ever perfectly willing all the time. The more you turn toward it, though, the more you will experience it and the freedom it brings. The following exercise will give you some structured practice.

Exercise: Practicing Willingness

1. Think of a situation that you will face relatively soon and that will create emotions—perhaps seeing a difficult person or being offered tempting food.

2. Now think of an emotion or sensation that you find difficult to sit with, that you think will arise in the situation, and that you would like to practice willingness to experience. Next, choose a length of time that you are willing to experience it. For example, you might choose to experience the feeling of deprivation, or the feeling of boredom, for 10 minutes.

3. Notice how you feel as you go into the situation in which you have decided to experience this uncomfortable emotion or sensation. Are you judging? Nervous? Resentful? Hopeful? Just notice the feelings; don't try to change them.

4. When you begin to feel the emotion or sensation you are practicing with, start timing yourself. As the time passes, keep track of your levels of willingness and how the emotion changes over time. What do you want to do in the face of this

emotion or sensation? How does your urge to act change over time? What actions do you choose to take, and what emotions arise as you act or don't act?

5. If you wish, once you have finished your time, you can switch to being willful. If it's acceptable in the moment, choose to do an action you held off from during your practice. If you do, notice how you feel before and afterward. Compare your period of willingness practice with a return to willfulness. What is your experience of emotion plus willingness? What is your experience of emotion plus willfulness?

♥

Honest Willingness

Here's a pitfall to be mindful of: are you practicing willingness to increase your flexibility, or instead to try yet another strategy to control the way you feel? If we use willingness and acceptance as attempts to control the way we feel, to feel less intensely, or to feel better, then we're not truly practicing willingness and acceptance. There is a difference between acting "willing" in the service of feeling less pain (which isn't really acceptance at all; it's an avoidance strategy) and practicing radical acceptance in the service of living life fully. In reality, acceptance may initially engender pain, especially if we've been running from pain. Honest acceptance includes practicing radical acceptance—returning when your mind moves away from acceptance, and adopting an attitude of honest willingness. For example, you can accept that you cannot continue to eat as you currently eat if you want to learn to manage emotions. And you can adopt a stance of acceptance and return your mind toward acceptance when you experience urges to avoid feeling by eating.

Right now, check in with yourself. Are you willing to participate in the process of feeling emotions without using food to cope, as well as returning your mind toward this goal whenever you move toward unhealthy habitual behaviors? Are you willing to change your relationship with food?

Exercise: Noticing Feelings and Practicing Acceptance

For this exercise, choose a situation you'll soon encounter where emotions will come up for you. Then, while you are in the situation and the feelings come up, practice noticing them without judgment. Practice bringing awareness to all emotions that arise, and honestly consider how willing or unwilling you are to sit with these emotions. Next, notice sensations and urges that accompany each emotion. After the experience, briefly note how you practiced acceptance. (Note this is a modified version of the emotional SIFTing process you learned in chapter 1.)

Situation: Write down the facts about an event or person that led to emotional reactions.

Interpretations: Did you notice **interpretations** or thoughts that relate to your experience?

Emotions and willingness: List any **emotions** you are experiencing and their intensity on a scale of nearly none (1) to extremely intense (10). For each emotion, also note your **willingness** on the same scale, with 1 being extreme unwillingness and 10 being complete willingness.

Feelings in my body: What feelings or sensations do you experience in your body?

Tendencies and urges: What **tendencies** or urges show up? Are you pulled to pursue particular actions?

How I am practicing acceptance: What skills or qualities did you call on to practice acceptance in the moment?

Here's an example:

Situation: Went to a friend's birthday dinner at my favorite restaurant, where I recently overate for emotional reasons. Felt anxious about potentially emotionally eating. I also felt quite angry over a recent conflict with my brother.

Interpretations and thoughts: I don't want to dwell on the fight with my brother. If feelings come up about my brother, I can accept them and bring myself back to the moment. It's okay to have urges to eat for emotional reasons; cravings don't have to dictate my behavior.

Emotions and willingness:

1. Anxiety—50, Willingness—80: I felt anxious about eating though pretty willing to feel anxious.

2. Anger—70, Willingness—20: I really didn't want to feel angry.

3. Joy—60, Willingness—90: I was happy to see friends, though I was a tiny bit unwilling to seem overly happy.

Feelings in my body: I recall feeling tension in my head and chest when I think about the fight. My heart raced a bit as I look at the menu.

Tendencies and urges: I was pulled to order what I enjoyed last time and to complain to my friends about the fight with my brother.

How I practiced acceptance: I nonjudgmentally noticed my emotions, thoughts, and feelings. I accepted them without trying to wish they weren't there. I practiced relaxing my face and body and accepting the discomfort of not ordering dessert when I wasn't physically hungry.

♥

We all struggle with significant challenges in life, and we may have adopted inefficient strategies for coping with these challenges, such as avoiding difficult emotions. When we increase our willingness around our experience, we become able to drop our sense of suffering and reach new heights.

Practicing Acceptance in Your Breath

I don't want to underemphasize the difficulty of practicing acceptance and willingness. To begin, it may be helpful to "practice acceptance with your breath"—that is, practice breathing in a manner that embodies acceptance, and then notice what happens with your mind. I noticed that when I pack or unpack from my frequent travels, and feel irritated or worried about time, I sound like I'm gasping for air, and when I breathe rhythmically, I feel more at ease. Sharon Salzberg, a remarkably practical meditation teacher and one of America's leading insight meditation teachers, explains that placing the body in a meditative sitting position is one of the best ways to practice meditation, because when the body is relaxed and stable, the mind will follow. When we hyperventilate and tense our facial muscles, we strengthen our anxiety response.

Mindful breathing relates to the practice of acceptance in several ways. When you move away from acceptance, you will generally experience a change in the depth and rate of your breathing. For example, when you are angry, you may notice your breath coming out in short bursts. When we face challenges, our breathing often becomes constricted; paying attention to our breathing and deepening and slowing it can facilitate acceptance and willing action. One way to practice accepting the present moment is by bringing complete awareness to your breath, one breath at a time. This is called *mindful breathing*. Breathing is available to us anywhere and anytime, and it can serve as a reminder to accept *this* moment with *this* breath—in essence, to accept the here and now.

When you focus awareness on your breath, you will notice urges to move your attention away from your breath—for example by following your thoughts or emotions. When this happens, you can choose to bring your attention back to your breath. Just as learning to practice acceptance in other ways entails noticing when we have moved away from acceptance and choosing to return to it, breathing with awareness entails noticing when our attention moves away and having the willingness to gently escort our awareness back to the breath. Gentleness and a willingness to return, again and again, are important—forcing the mind to return to the breath with an attitude of hostility and choosing to engage with interesting thoughts rather than attend to the breath are both ways of choosing nonacceptance over acceptance of the present moment.

Exercise: Mindful Breathing

To get a sense of what mindful breathing is like, read the instructions below, and then set a timer for anywhere from 5 to 15 minutes to practice. When you have finished, take a few moments to remember what you noticed as you were practicing.

1. Settle into a comfortable sitting position, with your spine erect. You may sit cross-legged if this is comfortable, with your knees below your hips, or sit upright in a chair, with your legs uncrossed and your feet resting flat on the floor. Your hands should rest comfortably on your knees, palms facing upward; this embodies openness.

2. You may focus your attention on a single point on the floor or ahead of you. Or you may close your eyes if that feels comfortable.

3. To begin, bring your awareness to physical sensations, such as your seat resting on the floor or your hands contacting your knees. Spend several moments paying attention to sensations in your body. In noticing sensations, we are simply observing with acceptance, one moment at a time, rather than thinking thoughts such as "Ugh, that pain in my knee will never go away." (Though if that thought comes, notice it without judgment and label it as a thought, and bring your attention back to sensations.) If you notice tension in your face, neck, or shoulders, relax those muscles.

4. Now move your awareness to the sensation of the breath in your body. Notice your breath as you inhale and as you exhale. Notice sensations of the breath moving in through your nostrils to your abdomen. Notice sensations of your breath as your abdomen expands like a balloon on the inhale and deflates on the exhale. Observe the breath moving up through

your diaphragm. In noticing, you are in a sense letting the breath breathe itself, rather than forcing it or willing it in any way.

5.   Your mind will wander away from your breath. That is what minds do. When your mind wanders, accept the wandering with kindness and compassion, and return your mind to participating fully in breathing.

♥

If you'd like to experiment with mindful breathing, you may practice it in situations where you struggle with acceptance, and notice what happens when you begin "accepting with the breath." For example, say that you are facing a plate of comfort food, knowing you are about to eat because you're feeling sad and not because you're hungry. In lieu of getting caught up in wishing that reality was different (for instance, that you had more willpower or weren't so sad), practice contacting reality as it is, relaxing your face and body and breathing mindfully as you notice what is in the moment.

When we practice like this, attending to the breath is not intended to distract or move us away from what lies before us. Rather, the breath may help us make contact with and accept the fact that we have choices. Breathing deeply and actively choosing which actions to pursue is very different from engaging in habitual, mindless behaviors. In one of her talks, Sharon Salzberg described attending to the breath as analogous to noticing an old friend in a large crowd: the breath may serve as a friendly reminder of our freedom to accept the moment and choose our actions consciously. Jon Kabat-Zinn (1990, 2) beautifully explains, "In this learning process we assume from the start that as long as you are breathing, there is more right with you than there is wrong, no matter how ill or hopeless you may feel."

Now that we've explored the value in acceptance, let's get a sense of why acceptance is the only viable choice.

The Heaviness of Nonacceptance

Eating to avoid emotion may be a deliberate strategy or a habitual pattern that is almost unconscious. In other words, you may experience an emotion, wish to control it, and, consciously or not, use food to avoid or alter it, implicitly reinforcing the notion that you just can't cope with your feelings.

Experiential avoidance, or attempts to avoid, suppress, or change negative events, including feelings, thoughts, and bodily sensations, underlies both emotional suffering (Hayes et al. 1996) and emotional eating.

Pain is a part of living. We are all faced with difficult emotions, painful memories, and obstacles. Many individuals describe their struggle with emotions as greater than their experience of physical pain. Dissatisfaction with one's shape and size may include a combination of emotional and physical discomfort. How do you cope with uncomfortable thoughts, feelings, and sensations?

Avoidance and control strategies can bring advantages. Our ancestors survived, in part, by taking precautions and gaining some degree of control over their situations. These coping strategies are thus in our DNA, and they are, in themselves, neither good nor bad. They are, however, sometimes ineffective in our daily lives. When are attempts to control our situations effective? If we need to concentrate on an important project, it is effective if we remove distractions. If we want to lose weight, it is useful if we limit the amount of sweets and processed fatty foods in the home. But attempts to control situations often fail, and *this usually happens when they are too rigid and/or when we try to use them in situations where they will not work.* For example, if you decide to pursue a highly restrictive diet in which you drastically reduce your intake of calories, you are likely to binge at some point because you will feel deprived. Control is also not feasible when we try to radically alter inalterable aspects of the body, such as the aging process. The next exercise is designed to give you some practice discerning when control strategies might be effective and when they might not be.

Exercise: Control or Let Go?

1. Spend a moment writing about or thinking of three examples of situations where your efforts at control seem not to work.

2. Taking each situation in turn, think of aspects you can control and aspects you cannot.

For example:

1. I can't control the fact that I experience food cravings.

   I can't control what other people think of me.

   I can't totally control how much I enjoy various activities.

2. I can make sure I purchase only healthy food items for my home, but I cannot control what my family members or guests choose to bring over.

   I can do my best to be a nice person and be myself, but I cannot control the fact that other people may or may not like me.

   I can pursue activities I tend to enjoy and that often make me feel better, but I cannot control how much I enjoy them on any particular day, nor can I guarantee that they will dramatically improve my mood.

♥

You Can't Turn Off Feelings

I love pithy sayings and here is my favorite: the problem is the solution. In other words, the problem is the way we try to get rid of feelings, not the experience of feeling itself. For example, if you struggle with panic, the actual feeling of anxiety will likely not handicap you as much as the behaviors you use to avoid panic, such as avoiding traveling, staying close to home, and overeating. A more helpful strategy is to experience those feelings, rather than trying to turn them off.

Certain strategies we employ to "fix" our feelings will inevitably cause us to feel them more intensely. Even the proverbial "control freak" will often fail when it comes to managing his emotions—you can organize your closets and subdue your children, but it is a lot harder to suppress your own inner life. Still, most of us try to *fix* our feelings. Who wants to feel fat, anxious, sad, or lonely? But our best efforts to subdue emotional pain often create additional suffering.

Exercise: Letting Go of Strategies to Avoid

1. Take a moment to think about ways you have tried to manage your emotions. Have you ever *avoided* the pain of being alone by keeping the television on, incessantly snacking, or using other avoidance behaviors? List as many strategies as you can that you have used to try to avoid or change your feelings.

2. What are the feelings you find most challenging to experience?

3. How might you practice accepting those feelings?

♥

Imagine that you are wearing your favorite pair of suede shoes, and you are walking down the street on your way to an important meeting. Suddenly, it starts to pour. You wait under an awning for several minutes, but wishing the rain away or remaining under the awning will not change the weather. You wait and worry and become physically tense. Your shoes will be ruined! But if you continue to wait and miss your meeting, the lost opportunity may equal the cost of several pairs of shoes.

Trying to control emotions is like trying to keep your shoes dry in a rainstorm. You may try, and certain techniques may even work in the short term—if you are caught in a rainstorm, it may be useful to step inside for some time. But what if you chose to walk—even to dance—in the rain? What if the deluge became part of your day, an anecdote for the meeting, something (among the many things life throws at you) that couldn't stop you?

We can't control our emotions any more than we can control the weather. Let's try this: Get really happy right now. Tough, isn't it? Try harder! What do you notice? Joy, sadness, confusion, loss—none of these can be turned on or off at our command. Willpower is simply not helpful here. In fact, efforts to switch melancholy into the "all joy, all the time" channel will generally magnify your sadness into real misery. Why set yourself up? Why "fail" at something that is not possible?

Mark's Story

Mark was diagnosed with attention deficit disorder (ADD) as a child. Understandably, he still struggles with organization and concentration. Mark works in sales, and given his ADD, he has strategically developed a plan to overprepare for meetings, thoroughly considering any potential obstacles.

One day on the way to a high-stakes meeting, Mark began to sweat. He tried to force himself to stop sweating by thinking about how humiliating it would be to be visibly dripping in front of his colleagues. This only led to more sweating. Worse, Mark felt so uncomfortable and anxious that he actually bought himself a large cold beer and a cheeseburger, despite the facts that he was on his way to a business meeting and has high cholesterol.

Mark's efforts to manage his anxiety and control his body were backfiring, and it wasn't the first time. He had a very well-conceived plan in place to handle meetings, but he still felt exhausted before and after important meetings. He increasingly tried to soothe himself with comfort foods, television, and alcohol. As you can imagine, the more effort he invested in controlling his body and avoiding his anxiety, the more anxious he actually felt and the less efficient he was in his work. And on the day I've just described, the more he sweated emotionally, the more he sweated physically—a strong metaphor for how ineffectual our attempts to control the uncontrollable can be.

Hiding Feelings Causes You to Feel More

While you may inhibit the ways you express an emotion, physiologically you experience increased sensations in parallel with any attempt to suppress your emotions (Gross and Levenson 1997). For example, if you try to avoid feeling anxious, you may reduce the look of panic on your face to some degree, but your heart rate will increase as a result of your trying to fake calmness. So inhibiting your expression of negative emotions does not provide relief from your experience of the feeling, but does the opposite. Researchers (e.g., Wegner, Quillian, and Houston 1996) also suspect that trying to inhibit emotions limits your ability to organize information. Think about it: if you're focused on managing your expression, it's difficult to concentrate on and attend to what's happening around you. In Mark's situation, he may sometimes be so attuned to his attempt to appear calm that he fails to notice how engaged his colleagues are with his presentation. Suppressing emotions may also affect your relationships with others. If you rigidly control your expression, will people in your life be aware of your struggle? And with your attention absorbed in managing how you appear, will you have much of a chance of seeing what is happening with them? Not likely, and the combined result is that you will probably feel more and more isolated and less likely to elicit or express supportive and loving behavior.

Feel Less, Eat More?

How does suppressing emotion lead to increased eating of comfort foods? One possibility is that the act of suppression is itself emotionally depleting. You may be expending energy on stifling your feelings, leaving you with few resources when it comes to monitoring food (Vohs and Heatherton 2000). Interestingly, if you are not on a diet, you are less likely to indulge, as there is less pressure surrounding food choices.

So here is the sequence: You start feeling sad. You don't express the emotion, but try to stop feeling it. You now have less control when it comes to choosing what you eat and are more likely to eat unhealthy comfort foods. Then, you feel guilt when you do turn to comfort foods—another negative emotion! Any bets on what happens when you suppress the guilt? When you maintain rigid standards of perfection, or are not willing to accept yourself as you are, food serves as a temporary escape (Heatherton and Baumeister 1991), but escaping once makes it that much more likely you'll be driven to seek escape again, and again, forgetting that this strategy doesn't actually work in the long term.

So what might happen if you didn't need to escape your self with food? What might happen if you compassionately acknowledged and addressed your sadness?

No Body Is Perfect

If you have a tendency to be perfectionistic, or are unwilling to accept your body, you will always find imperfections. Tara Brach (2003), a clinical psychologist who specializes in teaching self-acceptance, writes in her seminal book, *Radical Acceptance* "Imperfection is not our personal problem—it is a natural part of existing." Not being willing to accept imperfection creates imperfection. Inflexible preoccupation with your body shape keeps you struggling around food—and often leads to eating disorders (Fairburn 2008). When you define yourself by your shape and are unwilling to accept certain aspects of the way you are, you are likely to resort to harsh efforts to control your body by restricting your food or by overexercising. Ironically, rigid dieting may lead to loss of control over eating—and this happens for both psychological and biological reasons. Many people tend to overeat after skipping a meal or ending a restrictive diet: both the body and the mind seek to compensate for the deprivation.

What have you tried in your attempts to change your shape or size? Has any approach led to the desired goal, or did it lead to another futile quest for perfection? Consider what you think you may achieve in your quest for perfection. Personal appearance may seem more controllable than other aspects of life; perhaps that is why it is so tempting an avenue for self-improvement.

Anne's Story

Anne spent every morning on the stair climber for an hour. She'd run to her job, skip lunch, and return to the gym after work to lift weights and run. Did the extra workout boost her confidence? It did not.

In her free time, she'd study restaurant reviews and select places to dine. Dinner was her time to savor the food she craved. Anne spent nearly as much time on her looks as she spent at her job. She was her own full-time makeover coach. She spent hours a day on her hair, makeup, and clothing selection. But what was the payoff for all this effort? Did Anne actually feel any better than she had when she wore jeans or sweatpants and a T-shirt to her college classes? Not really.

In fact, the more Anne pursued "perfection," the less contented she felt. What was Anne running to, or escaping from? What feelings were pursuing her? Her time was so consumed with her appearance that she was able to dodge her emotions, at least temporarily. And there were other benefits. Anne did earn some positive attention from others. She was often asked on dates, even though she couldn't say she felt good about herself. The feelings she was trying to avoid always made themselves known in the form of a nagging unhappiness. Anne's worries about her appearance distracted her from the intrusive thoughts that there was something wrong with her.

In therapy, Anne engaged in an exercise called *mirror exposure* (G. Wilson 2002). She nonjudgmentally observed and described the entirety of what she saw in the mirror. She shifted from automatically seeing her body through a perfectionistic, judgmental lens to developing acceptance of the basic, true facts about her appearance. When Anne learned to accept her appearance and—just as important—to realize that she was more than her appearance, she began to feel peace. Through learning helpful ways to regulate emotions, developing flexibility and willingness to be in the moment, and exploring what really mattered, Anne finally gained a sense of ease.

Anne is not alone in her struggles with how she looks. People of varying sizes and shapes wrestle with accepting their bodies, especially in our youth-oriented, media-dominated world, in which the ideal shape for women is seemingly pencil-thin. Interestingly, overconcern with shape and weight often occurs independent of the culturally defined attractiveness of one's actual shape and weight (Eldredge and Agras 1996). In other words, even people who look like they should be happy with their shape and weight (by our cultural standards) are often unhappy with their shape and weight. In our culture, individuals whose weight is in the healthy range often wish to weigh less, and others judge themselves based on their shape and relationship with food more than by their relationships, hobbies, work, and family. Much of this anguish is in vain: the pattern of body fat distribution is largely a factor of genetics (Bouchard 1995); furthermore, the body tends to maintain a particular set point, making it difficult to drastically modify weight (Keesey 1995). In other words, you can't really change your waist to hip ratio—at least, not without surgery, and often not even with it—and your body has its own reasons for maintaining your weight and shape within certain parameters.

If excessive concern regarding shape and appearance is generally unhelpful, and magnifies the weight of weight in your life, what does appropriate concern look like? Of course, it is important to problem solve if you have difficulties around food and eating, but there is a difference between problem solving and obsessive or compulsive thoughts and actions. Everybody checks their body to some extent, but people who obsess about their appearance may scrutinize their bodies in a way that maintains suffering. Many people compare themselves to models and actresses who must conform to a certain standard or lose their livelihood (and who endure starvation, excessive exercise, and surgery to maintain their looks). Often, we compare ourselves to a select group of remarkably thin or "beautiful" people (as determined by strict modern standards) rather than the average person or every other person we see. Consider for a few moments your own body-checking habits:

- How often do you check your weight?

- How often do you look in the mirror?

- Do you observe yourself as a whole? Or do you scrutinize certain parts?

- Do you notice with critical eyes or kind eyes?

- What are you looking for when you check your body?

- Do you ever feel better after studying your body?

Exclusively focusing on parts is avoiding the whole—your body as a whole, your life as a whole. We may gaze at ourselves critically, like judges at a beauty contest, or lovingly, like a museumgoer in front of a curvaceous female nude. We are all beautiful in unique ways. Artists know this; those with calipers and scales miss the point. Mirrors are misleading, and what one sees depends a lot on how one looks at them (Fairburn 2008). We are seldom entirely objective when we look at ourselves.

Some people who struggle with their shape cope by avoiding looking in the mirror, forming intimate relationships, going to the beach, or buying new clothes. People may avoid weighing themselves or acknowledging their weight as a health concern. Some waver between extreme concern about weight and complete avoidance of the issue, like Joel.

Joel's Story

Joel would spend hours tanning, picking out expensive clothes, working with a personal trainer, and following a rigid diet—or he'd flip to the opposite extreme. When he wasn't being "good," he would wear old sweats, grow a scraggly beard, cancel his gym membership, and eat anything and everything. His friends marveled that the Joel they saw could weigh either 170 pounds or 250 pounds; he was rarely in between. Some probably wondered whether Joel was being kind to himself or to his body and whether this tortured ambivalence was sustainable.

When Joel's yoga teacher shared the mantra "You have a body but you are not your body," something shifted for Joel. He practiced whispering to himself gently when judgmental thoughts came up, "You have a body; you are not your body." He found that reminding himself to accept his shape, and to also accept that he was more than his weight, was helpful in maintaining balance in both weight and life.

Summary

We've spent this chapter learning about control and avoidance as coping mechanisms. When it comes to our feelings, research (and our own experience) shows these strategies are worse than ineffective: they actually backfire on us and magnify our suffering. Instead, acceptance is the only viable path to coping with pain and distress and experiencing life in full. In this chapter, you had the opportunity to practice experiencing willingness and acceptance around some issues you find painful. You learned to breathe mindfully, using your breath to experience acceptance and to remind you what that experience feels like. You may have had some insights into the things you avoid or try to control and the ways those strategies are or are not working for you. The movement from old ways of coping to newer ones can feel dangerous—research shows we more often choose a painful occurrence we're familiar with over a less painful, but new and unpredictable one (Badia, Harsh, and Abbott 1979). Be bold, and be gentle with yourself. Practice, but don't hold yourself to a standard of perfection. You *can* continually choose to accept your thoughts, feelings, sensations, and current situation. The switch to acceptance may *seem* exhausting, but you will find that it actually increases your vitality.

Chapter 3

MINDFUL MOMENTS

Usually we feel that there's a large problem and we have to fix it. The instruction is to stop. Do something unfamiliar. Do anything besides rushing off in the same old direction, up to the same old tricks.

—PEMA CHÖDRÖN

Imagine that you agree to participate in a research study and at times throughout the day, you are asked what you are doing, what you are thinking, and how you are feeling. You might think that what you are doing would determine how you feel. You may predict you'd feel happier at the beach than in a business meeting. Harvard researchers checked in with 2,250 adults through iPhone applications, asking them numerous times a day, "Are you thinking about something other than what you are currently doing?" The researchers found that when people spent time thinking about events other than those occurring in the moment, they were less happy; wandering minds are unhappy minds (Killingsworth and Gilbert 2010). *Thinking* was more related to happiness than was doing—in other words, when your mind is not on whatever it is you're doing, it's hard to experience joy or purpose. Thinking comes at an emotional cost. In this chapter you will learn to be where you are both when you eat and more generally.

Practicing *mindfulness* may affect your eating in several ways. It can increase your awareness of your emotions, thoughts, and sensations, and you may find yourself more able to experience life events without using food to cope. Also, if you practice eating mindfully, you are more aware of your eating. Many people who struggle with food describe a loss of control when eating. Eating mindfully is a way of regaining flexibility and awareness. When you eat mindfully, you notice what you are eating bite by bite and you are able to experience more pleasure and satisfaction. Throughout this chapter and those that follow, mindfulness serves as a foundation from which to observe emotions, eating, and thinking and, more generally, to participate wholeheartedly in life. In this chapter, we will explore how to begin to notice judgments, practice mindfulness, observe your state of mind, and bring mindful attention to both eating and your experience of hunger.

What Is Mindfulness?

Mindfulness is a core practice in the Buddhist tradition and other Eastern meditative traditions. But mindfulness is not tied to any specific religion; it describes a quality of attention consistent with all religions. For example, theological historians describe a meditative tradition present in Judaism since biblical times (Kaplan 1985). When you practice mindfulness, you practice living with intention. It's the opposite of being a slave to habit and indulging impulses.

In 1979, the Stress Reduction and Relaxation Program at the University of Massachusetts Medical Center began integrating mindfulness into Western medical practice. Since then, mindfulness has been extensively researched and found useful in treating a wide range of both medical and psychological problems. In his seminal book on mindfulness, Jon Kabat-Zinn (1990) introduced an exercise in which you practice eating a single raisin with full awareness (I've included a version of this exercise at the end of this chapter). Eating a raisin with full attention illustrates the manner in which we may slow down and savor even the most banal food. Mindfulness is helpful for people who struggle with both eating (e.g., Safer, Telch, and Chen 2009; Thich Nhat Hahn and Cheung 2010) and sitting with difficult emotions (Linehan 1993a; Hayes, Strosahl, and Wilson 1999).

Practicing mindfulness is like turning on the lights in your life—though mindfulness is not instantaneous. You don't *get* mindful; you *practice* mindfulness over time, building skill and patience. Mindfulness increases mental flexibility, opening new options to you, and actually thickens the middle prefrontal cortex of your brain, facilitating acting in accordance with your goals (Siegel 2010). However, mindfulness is not about achieving anything, as the practice is based on acceptance. Still, many people notice that mindfulness may reduce suffering, increase joy, and allow us to experience reality as it is in each moment. (Linehan 1993b)

How does mindfulness reduce suffering, increase joy, and facilitate contact with reality? As we've touched on in previous chapters, we can really suffer if we are not only awash in the pain of the present, but also consumed by past problems and potential difficulties in the future. Learning to sit with the now can free us from that additional weight, drastically reducing our suffering. In the same way, mindfulness increases joy—it is virtually impossible to enjoy something if we aren't fully in contact with it. If you are on vacation worrying the trip will end, are you relishing this moment? Finally, if we aren't fully present in each moment, we may find ourselves responding to events that aren't actually occurring. A good way to understand this is to consider a common mindless experience—say, waking up on a Saturday (your day off) concerned you overslept and are late for work. You may even find yourself getting dressed hurriedly before you realize, "Hey, it's Saturday!" You may find yourself in similar situations throughout the day when you are caught in the alarms of your mind, unconscious of the reality of the moment.

Mindfulness Defined

Mindfulness is the awareness that stems from *paying attention, on purpose, in the moment* (Kabat-Zinn 2003). Mindfulness practice entails paying attention in a particular way to one's emotions, thoughts, sensations, and experiences. It requires letting go of our tendencies to judge and control. We all possess the capacity for mindfulness; we simply have to bring ourselves back to this home within us. The practice includes choosing a stance of openness and honoring our experiences with compassionate awareness. One component of the practice is self-regulation, allowing you to direct attention toward the present moment; another component is a stance of curiosity, openness, and acceptance (Bishop et al. 2004). Our minds may veer off from the present, and when we are mindful of this we kindly shift our focus back to now.

Mindfulness can be (and has been) defined fairly precisely, but it is best understood experientially, through practice. We can talk a lot about the mechanics of skiing, but you won't get a real feel for the experience until you actually ski. So I'll briefly break down Jon Kabat-Zinn's formulation of mindfulness (paying attention, on purpose, in the moment, without judgment) and then you can begin practicing. You'll find that being mindful is about *being,* not doing or figuring out.

Paying attention on purpose means you are focusing on what lies before you. When you practice mindfulness, you attend to only one thing at a time. You may shift your attention from the sky to the sound of birds, but this is quite different from the fragmenting quality of multitasking, where your attention is split so it's neither fully on the birds nor fully on the sky.

When you practice mindfulness you are neither avoiding nor grasping. You are letting go of attempts to control. This doesn't mean you don't care—quite the contrary; this quality reflects caring *wisely.* Mindfulness describes awareness *in this moment.* Of course, your mind may be accustomed to moving away from the moment. Minds jump around a lot, and it's a challenge to see clearly with a jumpy mind. It is, however, helpful to notice this jumpiness. When you notice that you aren't in the moment, that is itself a moment of noticing and an opportunity to begin again.

Mindfulness is noticing *without judgment.* What are judgments? When we make a judgment, we superimpose thoughts on facts. This may move us away from being aware moment to moment and can result in our overlooking important information. For example, thinking, "Sam didn't return my call. He hates me" is not mindful. We have no idea why Sam didn't return the call, and it doesn't really matter. The judgment "He hates me" narrows our attention and may get in the way of noticing the sunset before our eyes. I'll never forget a chief psychologist yawning during my job interview. I was sure I would not be hired. An observable yawn is factual, yet concluding he was unimpressed by me was a judgment. Days later, I was surprised to receive a job offer. Judgments, as this example suggests, can create unnecessary pain and can affect how you feel about both yourself and the people in your life. Anger generally occurs around judgments about how people "should" act.

Many of my clients argue that it's "normal" to judge. And yes, of course we all make judgments. The issue here is about how *effective* judgments are. At times, it is indeed helpful and effective to make snap judgments based on past experience. At other times, judgments pose problems, particularly when judgments are so habitual we fail to differentiate them from facts. Just because you think you are ugly does not mean that you are unattractive. Mindfulness includes awareness that thoughts are not facts (we'll explore this concept more in chapter 6). It may be useful to replace judgments with facts or statements of preference or consequence. For example, replace the judgment "I'm unattractive" with the statement of fact "Beauty is subjective." Replace "I'm a failure because I'm single" with the statement of preference "I would like to be in a loving relationship"; replace "I can't change" with "Change may take time."

Many people have held particular judgments about their bodies, emotions, and eating for a long time. These judgments may seem so true given how long they have been with you that they feel real. Would you be willing to bring your attention to judgments that seem familiar and spend a moment noticing they are judgments? The following exercise is designed to help you practice this around the issues of food, emotions, and the body.

Exercise: Noticing Judgments

Write down some beliefs you notice often in relation to food, your emotions, and/or your body. In which situations does each thought arise? If the thought is a judgment, replace it with a more accurate fact or a statement of preference. Any time you encounter a judgment, you may use this quick exercise both to understand when and where the judgment comes up and to replace it with a more effective statement of fact or preference.

Where and When	Judgment	Statement of Fact or Preference

♥

Cultivating a Mindfulness Practice

You may practice mindfulness formally or informally. Many people find a combination helpful. In practicing mindfulness formally, you may learn to notice the usual places your mind goes; this can pave a path to bringing mindful awareness to other parts of your day. When practicing informally, you bring present-moment awareness to routine activities throughout the day.

Formal Practice

Cultivating a formal practice is a bit like scheduling an appointment with yourself to practice mindfulness. Formal practices may involve taking time away from your regular daily activities to sit and be aware of your breath. You may decide to sit in a particular place, in a chair or on a cushion on the floor, from seven to seven fifteen every morning. It's helpful to sit in a way that is conducive to practice. Sitting in full lotus position may be impossible, yet sitting too comfortably may lead to you (or your feet) falling asleep. Find a middle path. Find a location where you are not distracted, or choose something nondistracting to focus on—sitting in front of a computer or clutter may fill you with the desire to "do" rather than "be." (If you would like to begin a practice and have difficulty with follow-through, you may set an alarm to remind you to practice each morning, or sign up for e-mail reminders at habitforge.com.)

Informal Practice

An informal practice involves applying mindfulness to your life more flexibly yet still deliberately. This may include going to a concert and really listening, or turning off the TV, closing your book, putting the iPhone away, and sitting at the table to eat with complete awareness. You may practice mindfulness when you shower, listen to music, or talk with a friend. If you choose to practice talking with a friend mindfully, you fully participate in the conversation, noticing when distracting thoughts arise, observing thoughts without fighting or holding on to them, and returning your attention to your friend. If you decide to shower mindfully, you attend to the sensations in the shower (the water, the temperature, the feeling of soap in your hair); you are not engaging in worries about your business meeting. When that thought arises, notice it, and return your attention to the water pressure.

Eric's Story

Eric told me he could not stop thinking, and feelings were too painful. He numbed himself with marijuana, fast food, and alcohol. When I asked how these behaviors were working for him, he said, "They aren't." He had long considered himself a failure. He spent a lot of time and money trying to quiet his mind with loud music and mood-altering substances. And his mind got louder and his life got smaller. We discussed experimenting with mindfulness. Eric began to sit and meditate for three minutes each day at noon, and he also brought awareness to eating his dinner. After practicing for several months, he wouldn't say he felt better or liked slowing down—it still felt downright scary—but he noticed that, over time, he had become less afraid of his feelings and more aware of his thinking patterns. Eric is most proud of being less enslaved by habits. Some days are easier than others.

If you're willing, it may be helpful to commit to practicing mindfulness formally and/or informally for several weeks. Notice the experience. Mindfulness is a lot like weight training in that it requires consistent repeated efforts; over time, mindfulness changes the brain (e.g., Siegel

2010). As you consider starting a mindfulness practice, you may notice thoughts like "That's just not my personality; I can't be in the moment" and "I don't have time." Are those thoughts, or are they facts?

Exercise: Journaling Your Experience

Keeping track of your practices may both help you remember to practice and also provide you with information. You can use the following format to record how you practice mindfulness, whether formally or informally.

Date	How I Practiced	What I Noticed

Many people find that a combination of practicing formally for a specified period of time each day (even for five minutes) and practicing informally can be helpful. I find formal mindfulness practice more challenging than informal practice: I prefer to run around rather than sit quietly. Sitting formally has been a useful practice for me, and when sitting feels too difficult or sleep-inducing, I practice observing my breath while walking mindfully.

♥

How Are We Mindless in Our Eating?

For any number of reasons we may find ourselves distracted while eating. Research suggests that distraction during a meal both increases food intake during that meal and leads to increased food intake after the meal (Oldham-Cooper et al. 2011). Part of our experience of feeling full has to do with remembering that we ate, and it's difficult to recall eating when our focus has moved away from really noticing and tasting the food.

Multitasking

Often, as a result of learning or lifestyle, we are accustomed to TV dinners. And I don't mean instant dinners in little microwavable trays. I am referring to the pairing of TV (or another distraction, such as a book, computer, or newspaper) and food. Our attention is captivated by the screen or page and diverted from the food before us. The society we live in, which confuses multitasking with productivity, supports this kind of distracted eating. And it's understandable that, when we are busy, it is difficult to move away from work or other activities, slow down, and eat with complete awareness.

There may also be an emotional component to distracted eating. If we experience anxiety or guilt in the context of eating, we may find ourselves avoiding the emotions that arise during meals by occupying ourselves with other activities. If this resonates with your experience, mealtime may be an ideal time to really practice the willingness to notice and accept your feelings.

Eating Too Quickly

From an evolutionary perspective, eating quickly before the available food is consumed by others is adaptive. However—thankfully—as modern people our next meal may reasonably be available within minutes. Eating quickly often relates to busyness. When our attention is diverted from the act of eating, our eating speed increases (Andrade, Greene, and Melanson 2008). For many of us, eating has become a mechanical activity: we chew like we type, the faster the better. It's true that we are busy people, yet eating hurriedly may be analogous to driving too quickly: we are likelier to lose control. I notice that I tend to eat more quickly when I'm dining with a fast eater. It feels contagious, and slowing myself down requires awareness.

Again, eating quickly may also relate to trying to avoid emotions that arise while eating. Some patients have told me that on some emotional level, they feel that if they eat something "forbidden" quickly, it doesn't count. However, when we eat quickly to dodge our emotions, we may lose the opportunity to experience joy or other positive emotions in eating. And, of course, we may inadvertently eat too much.

Eating at the Fridge or on the Run

Eating on the road or at the counter is often associated with multitasking and eating too quickly. Consider for a moment the difference between sitting down to eat a meal at a restaurant and eating from a take-out container while you're standing with the fridge door open. It's hard to imagine you'll eat with full attention while standing in front of the refrigerator. It may be helpful to seek out a situation conducive to eating wisely—a nicely laid table, for example, rather than the driver's seat of your car.

Lack of Awareness of Satiety

For a host of reasons, it may be difficult for us to know much about our experience of hunger or our experience of feeling satiated. Brian Wansink describes in his book *Mindless Eating* (2010) how he and his colleagues devised a scenario where pipes below a dining table continuously refilled diners' soup bowls. People did not notice they were consuming three bowls of soup!

Eating is often influenced by emotional, social, and cognitive variables, rather than solely by physiological hunger. A history of dieting, overeating, and emotional eating can obscure our awareness of our physiological appetite. Often, we are most familiar with the extremes of hunger and satiety—the growling stomach and the faint feeling when we are famished, and then the distending fullness, when it feels difficult to breathe and our pants need to be unbuttoned.

Lack of Awareness of Our Emotions

If you are in the habit of eating to stop feeling, you may confuse emotional pain with hunger. As we saw in chapter 1, eating may serve as a way to avoid or escape emotions. When you bring awareness to your emotions, you may choose how to respond rather than habitually reacting.

Lack of Knowledge about What We're Eating

Many of us buy prepared meals or eat in restaurants. It may be difficult to find out nutritional information or control portion size. We can't really fully participate in the moment of eating when we don't know basic facts about what we're eating. Recently, several restaurants in my area began posting nutritional information. I was shocked that a piece of cake could have 800 calories! Still, this is valuable information from the point of view of mindfulness. Knowing what an item contains and how many calories it has means that we can accept the reality about that food and make a choice from there. And that choice doesn't necessarily have to be "too many calories—no cake for me." There is a wide middle ground between meticulously counting every calorie, or depriving ourselves of calorie-dense foods, and entirely avoiding thinking about the nutritional information in food and just going for it. Eating a piece of cake while obsessing over its calorie content is not very mindful. A more workable stance involves having general knowledge of what the food contains in terms of ingredients, nutrients, and calories; flexibility in attitude and judgment about the food; attention to portion size; and a willingness to slow down and savor taste.

Exercise: How Am I Mindless in My Eating?

Take out your notebook and bring to mind one or more instances of mindless eating in the last week.

1. Without judgment, factually describe the behaviors you've noticed or can remember that got in the way of eating with your full attention.

2. What emotions did you notice while eating unmindfully?

3. Describe briefly how mindless eating affected your experience.

♥

Larry's Story

Larry was busy. He worked, assisted his elderly parents, and was an avid golfer. Often, he ate at his desk, consuming his lunch in a maximum of four minutes while also checking his e-mail and, occasionally, returning calls. During a therapy session, we considered how his food was arranged and all the minute details involved in preparing the bread, deli meats, lettuce and pickles, chips, soda, and banana. He sat for several minutes appreciating the people involved in his lunch, including the farmers, shippers, and grocers. Generally, we fail to attend to the process as well as the sight, taste, smell, and feel of each bite of food. We feel too hurried to savor the moment in all its depth and complexity. When Larry brought attention to his lunches, he heightened both his enjoyment of the food and his satisfaction after eating. He noticed he felt full after mindfully eating a sandwich and did not need to also eat the banana and chips at lunch; he began saving them for later in the day. Slowing down also made him realize that his soda was too sweet and did not quench his thirst. Larry also sought more knowledge about what he was so speedily consuming. He thought the "#6" was a tasty take-out order at the deli. When he decided that, as part of his expanding awareness, he'd research the nutritional information of his sandwich, his mouth fell open: the three layers of corned beef, chopped liver, and Russian dressing in the #6 delivered more calories and cholesterol than his cardiologist recommended for the entire day. Acting on this awareness, he discovered he felt satiated by a sandwich with two layers of corned beef and dressing and liver on the side.

What Is Mindful Eating?

You can chomp your food, or you can cherish it. *Mindful eating* describes the practice of bringing your full awareness to your experience while eating. Have you ever noticed the discrepancy between the time and effort involved in food preparation and the speed of food consumption? Mindful eating cultivates both gratitude and gratification in eating.

Find a Seat

When I was in grade school, a teacher took us out to celebrate the end of the year at an ice cream store. Several people stood around eating. Mrs. Smiles (yes, that was her actual name) authoritatively instructed us, "My friends, we all need to find chairs. Animals eat while standing; *we* are kings." Just as it is helpful to adopt a posture conducive to formally practicing mindfulness, it's important to sit in a manner consistent with eating mindfully. Chairs are everywhere: take a seat!

Give Thanks

Taking a moment to notice your food before eating, and taking a moment to notice your sensations after eating, may bring meaning and even sanctity to a moment that you may associate with shame. I love reminding myself that food didn't just land on my plate and that I am so fortunate to be able to eat when so many people have too little food. This practice is not about judging ourselves or feeling undeserving or sorry for the hungry; it's about really noticing what lies before us, just for a moment. You may give thanks to a higher power, horticulture, Häagen-Dazs, or your host, if this is a helpful practice for you.

Take a Picture!

Maybe you thought food photography was just for foodies. Many programs designed to combat binge eating encourage keeping food logs, and a food record is an important tool for taking inventory and increasing awareness around food consumption. However, after a long day, it can be hard to remember precisely what we ate, and it's often hard to maintain food logs because of the time, energy, and potential shame involved. In a 2008 study, Lydia Zepeda and David Deal from the University of Wisconsin–Madison encouraged participants to photograph their food before consuming it. People who photographed food before eating it were forced to slow down and consider their choices before eating. Delaying eating to take a photograph provides a moment of opportunity to consider our emotions and urges before we act. A combination of slowing down, taking a picture (quick and easy if you have a camera in your phone), and reviewing your daily eating to notice emotional eating can be remarkably effective in increasing your range of choices about your eating.

Slow Down

You can practice mindfulness, no matter where you are or whom you are with, by *slowing down* as you eat. We begin to feel full only about twenty minutes after we have eaten our fill—it takes that much time before our brain and stomach can agree that we feel satiated. If we slow down, we can observe our degree of physiological hunger and eat more only if we are actually still hungry. Putting your fork down in between bites is a good way to slow down a bit. Eating more slowly will require that you cultivate acceptance and practice turning your mind back to the present moment when you have urges to eat too quickly, multitask while eating, or otherwise pay little attention to the meal.

Bring Awareness to Each Bite

Imagine that you are eating a salad with many ingredients—lettuce, tomato, avocado, turkey, feta cheese, corn, and a rich, creamy dressing. Do you notice the colors of the lettuce or the shapes of the tomato? Do you notice the various tastes in your mouth? Are you aware of each bite? Do you notice each distinct sight, taste, texture, smell, and sensation as you raise your fork to your mouth, chew, and swallow? If someone asked you to identify what you ate after a large forkful, would you be able to pinpoint the bit of corn in that particular bite? Often, we eat so quickly that it's difficult to attend to our eating. Again, it's interesting that it may take hours to prepare food that may then be gobbled up so quickly we hardly notice the taste of our efforts. Given that eating can be so enjoyable, why do we rush the process?

Exercise: A Single Mindful Bite

One way to practice eating mindfully is by eating a single food item (a marshmallow, a Hershey's Kiss, a raisin, a fresh strawberry, a mint, or some other bite-sized food of your choice) as though you have never seen or tasted it before, seeking full awareness in the present moment, without judgment. As with previous mindfulness practices, to do this one, assume a comfortable seated posture and set a timer for three to five minutes. Of course your mind may wander, and that is a moment to return to your food. (The first part of this exercise is inspired by Jon Kabat-Zinn 1990.)

1. See: Take the food you've selected and rest it in the palm of your hand. Spend some time fully observing it. You may notice the color, where the light hits it, and the features of its surface.

2. Touch: Touch the food with your finger, attending to its texture as you touch it. You may notice subtleties of its tactile qualities (soft or firm, tacky or slick, rough or smooth, moist or dry) as it sits between your fingers.

3. Smell: Bring the food below your nose and smell it. Try moving the food away from your nose and then back, bringing awareness to smells you may notice as you do so.

4. Taste: Place the food on your tongue, and just let it rest there for a while before you chew. Notice any tastes that arise before chewing begins. You may notice the urge to swallow or chew. Try moving the food to one side of your mouth and bringing your awareness to the sensation of it sitting against your teeth.

5. Chew: Begin to chew the food with deliberate attention. Notice tastes that emerge; notice the texture as it may change over time. Notice any urges to swallow and, when you do swallow, continue to bring deliberate attention to your thoughts, emotions, and sensations.

Now reflect on your experience, using your notebook to answer the following questions as briefly or expansively as you wish.

1. What did you notice when you ate in this very deliberate, attentive way?

2. How do you think this practice differs from the way you normally eat?

3. Would you be willing to practice eating a single meal or snack with mindful awareness? If so, describe the meal, the setting, and the ways you will practice attending to your food and your eating.

♥

Pay Attention to Nutrition

You may bring awareness to eating by learning more about what you consume. At times, people make decisions about food based on thoughts or feelings rather than facts. A client of mine, for example, convinced herself that a smoothie had fewer calories than a bagel and cream cheese and felt very deprived as she drank her smoothie while dreaming of a New York toasted bagel. When we reviewed the facts, we discovered the calories were comparable. It can be helpful to gather nutritional information by exploring the extensive food listings on www.livestrong.com or www.myfitnesspal.com, or by consulting with a professional.

Pay Attention to Your Appetite

It may be hard to truly know what hunger is (in a physiological sense) when so often we associate it with feeling an uncomfortable emotion. If you don't notice when you're hungry, how can you notice when you are full?

Mona described purchasing pretzels each time she passed the vending machine at work, rationalizing that she felt tired. "Tired" and "hungry" are different feelings, though eating often diminishes both. Many other feelings or circumstances prompt us to eat, and they obscure our experience of hunger. We may be prompted to eat when a coworker brings in brownies or we feel bored. We may decide how much to eat according to the amount we are served, even though portion sizes often vary depending on where we eat—and portion size may have little to do with our own experience of fullness. In this case, slowing down and tasting one bite at a time may help you get more in touch with how much food is filling, regardless of the portion before you.

Linda Craighead (2006) developed the concept of training people in appetite awareness. We can reorient ourselves to the whispers of our appetite by bringing mindful awareness to our levels of hunger and fullness and training ourselves to respond to *moderate* levels of hunger and *moderate* levels of satiety instead of the alarms of starvation or overeating. Again, we are practicing moving away from thinking in all-or-nothing terms— where hunger is "starving" and fullness is "stuffed." A more middle-ground approach involves attending to what moderate hunger and moderate fullness feel like and using those sensations to guide us.

It's important to eat when you notice moderate hunger. If you wait until you are starving, you may find yourself overeating. It's also important to respond to moderate levels of satiety rather than eating until you feel entirely full—remember, we often don't register fullness until twenty minutes after we've eaten our fill. The two work well together, but each is helpful on its own: even if you eat in response to an emotional cue for hunger, you may attend to cues of moderate fullness to stop overeating.

If you anticipate that noticing hunger or satiety signals will feel impossible due to habitual eating for emotional reasons, you may start out by setting up times to eat three meals and several snacks, so that you do not go for long periods without eating. Planning and scheduling creates a situation where eating is influenced by a plan rather than a mood. In preparing meals and snacks, choose your portions wisely and practice eating mindfully. Several practices noted earlier may similarly help you create conditions that foster eating in moderation, including sitting while eating, slowing down, and taking a picture, even mentally, before you eat. It can be difficult to eat in moderation when you eat habitually and according to emotions. Emotions may persuade you, for example, to take a second serving while you are still midbite. A reasonable plan can help you circumvent emotional reasoning.

Exercise: Mindfulness of Hunger and Fullness

If you would like to practice appetite awareness, you may grab a notebook and keep track of how hungry or full you are both when you start to eat and when you finish your meal. Practicing bringing awareness to your hunger and fullness may help you find your eating "sweet spot." Use the format below to record your observations of your hunger and fullness around a meal or snack. Use a scale from 1 to 7 (with 1 meaning totally famished and 7 meaning stuffed to the point you may need to loosen your belt) twice— once to record how you felt before you started eating, and once to record how you felt after eating. If you are taking photographs of your meals, you may also note this information alongside your food photos.

Time/ Place	Hunger Level Before (1–7)	Satiety Level After (1–7)	How Was I Mindful?	Observations

Mind Your Emotions

In addition to noticing physiological hunger, noticing your emotional landscape while eating provides important information. You may practice observing and labeling your emotions as you did in chapter 1.

Beyond noticing specific emotions, you may also notice when you find yourself in a place, or state of mind, where emotions govern. We all ride between various states of mind, and we can practice mindfully noticing the state we inhabit in any moment. No single state of mind is always ideal—the optimal state depends on the situation, as we'll discuss in the following section.

States of Mind

As we well know, eating can be influenced by emotions. Eating—and much of our thinking—may similarly be affected by our *state of mind*. When we are unaware of what our state of mind is, and of how it may be affecting our thoughts and feelings, we may act unmindfully in accordance with this inner state. Mindful awareness of our state of mind gives us more capacity to act with intention: if we discern that we are in an emotional state, we may choose to slow down and take extra care of ourselves; if we are exuberant, we may choose to enjoy the mood, but also to realize that plans made now might be overly optimistic; and so on.

Daniel Siegel (2010), clinical professor of psychiatry at UCLA School of Medicine, calls awareness of our inner workings *mindsight*. When you practice mindsight, you may notice that there are times you are in "reasonable mind," where logic governs; times you find yourself in "emotion mind," where decisions are ruled by emotions; and times you have the capacity to merge reason and emotion, arriving at a state called "wise mind" (Linehan 1993a).

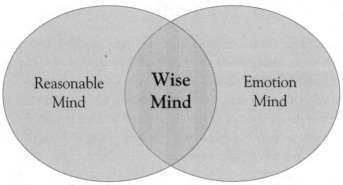

Figure 2: States of Mind

In *reasonable mind*, we make decisions intellectually, using facts to influence our choices (Linehan 1993a, 1993b). Operating in reasonable mind, we may make the decision to eat based on facts, such as "It's dinnertime." Similarly, in reasonable mind we might base a decision about where to live based on logistics.

In *emotion mind*, emotions govern our mind and behavior (Linehan 1993a, 1993b). We may be in emotion mind when we look at a painting or engage in intimacy. We may also be in emotion mind when we hit the snooze button even though we know we need to wake up. It's emotion mind that guides us to procrastinate on our work project by shopping on the Internet.

Of course, it isn't always that clear-cut. For example, if you were an art critic, you might be in reasonable mind when examining a painting. If you are prone to anxiety, you might be in reasonable mind in a moment of intimacy, analyzing your behavior or trying to evaluate your partner's experience. You may fluctuate between reasonable mind and emotion mind in the same situation. Similarly, you may begin eating based on reason and continue to indulge out of emotion. The aim of mindsight is to allow you to notice the state of mind you are in.

Wise mind describes the state of mind in which both emotion and reason join, perhaps creating a sense of intuition (Linehan 1993a, 1993b). An example might be when we're house-shopping and we visit an open house that makes sense reasonably—it's in an optimal location and within our budget—as well as emotionally—we like how it looks, and it feels like home. Head and heart coalesce when we are in wise mind; it is our internal compass. Certain situations call for reason, others call for emotion, and some decisions require the union of reason and emotion. Wise mind can facilitate making optimal decisions about such important matters as career, friends, and spiritual path.

At times, we may make decisions more wisely by consciously adding reason to emotion or emotion to reason. For example, if you are depressed, emotionally you feel tired and don't want to do anything. When you invite reason into your decision-making process, you consider how you will feel over time, or the fact that you may feel more energized by taking a walk. Or, if you are thinking about pursuing a project and reasonably you know it will take both time and money, you may call on emotion to get perspective about how you will feel engaging in the activity. Combining the two presupposes that you have been able to discern your dominant state of mind and therefore can more easily *choose not to act out of that state of mind*. For example, my lovely client Elaine was considering taking a course on teaching adult literacy to incarcerated populations. The course would take time and money, and Elaine is seventy-six years old and was concerned about the logistics. In our work, she mindfully considered the emotional experience of reading with an adult who had little freedom, and this persuaded her to move forward. She did not have to ignore her very reasonable concerns about time, money, and logistics, but she was able to decide that, on balance, these concerns were not enough to stop her.

So: mindfulness allows you to notice your state of mind and to make choices based on awareness. Are you in emotion mind when reasonable mind would actually be more appropriate? Noticing, "Hey, I'm in emotion mind," while you're trying to have a reasonable conversation about an emotional topic might reduce impulsive speech. Even labeling your state of mind "emotion mind" can help you access reasonable mind, because reasonable mind is what does the labeling. The following exercise will give you a sense of what it's like to notice state of mind.

Exercise: Noticing Your State of Mind

Grab a notebook and call to mind, as best you can, each of the following. Describe each situation nonjudgmentally (just the facts).

1.   A time you made a decision in emotion mind.

2. A time you acted in reasonable mind.

3. A time you used wise mind.

4. A time you found yourself in a state of mind that wasn't especially effective. Describe how you might have noticed your state of mind and practiced accessing alternative perspectives.

♥

Many people worry they don't have a "wise mind" or perceive themselves to be either overly logical or too emotional (Linehan 1993a). But all humans have a wise mind, and accessing it just takes practice. Marsha Linehan (1993a, 215) uses this analogy: "The fact that a patient cannot see her heart doesn't mean she doesn't have one."

Can you think back to a time when you made a wise-mind decision? It doesn't have to be a major decision. You may remember the time when you made an appointment with a physician even though you felt anxious because of your long-standing fear that you may have cancer. Though your emotion mind—your fear and anxiety—may have rationalized not making the appointment ("It's probably nothing"), perhaps your wise mind stepped in to say, "I should get it checked out anyway." When you notice, "I avoid medical appointments when I'm in emotion mind," you are more free to pursue wise-mind considerations the next time you have a health concern.

Wise mind may be hard to access when emotions are intense—if you are driving during a storm, it's hard to see a couple of feet ahead, let alone see your destination. You may need to slow down and use tools to keep yourself safe (to extend the driving metaphor: driving slowly, turning on your GPS, or even pulling over until the weather calms down) until you have the wherewithal to access wise mind. Keeping yourself safe while in emotion mind might include things like not having foods in the house that you tend to binge on and making sure you have a healthy stew or soup in your freezer at all times for when you feel like just eating ice cream for dinner. (We'll spend a lot of time on the subject of coping with intense emotions in chapter 7.)

Many people experience wise mind as a place of calm within a storm. Still, slowing down to contemplate what is wise can feel scary, since it requires sitting with a sense of uncertainty. Practice helps. The following exercise will give you some practice accessing wise mind.

Exercise: Accessing Wise Mind

Use the following questions to work your way toward a decision that requires both head and heart.

1. Identify a current situation where you would like to make a decision or take an action using wise mind.

2. Now sit somewhere quiet (or where you won't be disturbed) for a few minutes.

3. What decision or action are you pulled toward in this situation? Does that decision or action arise from emotion mind or reasonable mind?

4. What possible decisions or actions can you think of that would reflect another state of mind (i.e., if you are pulled toward reasonable-mind actions, what does your emotion mind say, and vice versa)?

5. Can you think of an action or decision that is a synthesis of emotion and reason and that your intuition feels drawn to? This may be an action or decision that is rooted in wise mind.

♥

Eating, Feeling Fat, and States of Mind

Habits, including habits around food and eating, are routine and may seem almost automatic; mindful awareness is a freedom from routine. Thus if you find your eating habits are causing you distress, it may be useful to practice noticing your emotions when you eat. Noticing can give you enough distance from your habits to provide you with flexibility. If you find yourself preoccupied with food or your body, bringing attention to your state of mind around these issues can also help. Both practices— noticing emotion and state of mind—can provide you with more awareness and more freedom to make healthy decisions, by allowing you to be more present in the moment.

When you use reasonable mind, you may eat when you are hungry or eat at a particular time—say, in the morning—even if you don't feel hungry, so that you won't feel famished later. Reasonable mind may direct you to start eating when your hunger level is moderate and to stop eating when you experience a moderate level of fullness.

How might wise mind affect your eating choices? Perhaps you are at a birthday party and, reasonably, you know you are trying to cut back on sweets. Everyone else is eating birthday cake, and your host is not taking no for an answer. In wise mind, you might take a mindful bite or two of the cake, noticing any permissive thoughts you may have, such as "Now that I've already had a bit of sugar, why not enjoy the parfaits and truffles too?" Yet you may still make the choice not to indulge in more sweets, instead simply noticing your feelings of craving, which will eventually pass. Alternatively, you may be in wise mind when you politely but firmly say no to the host and notice a feeling of pride and strength.

Reasonable mind may be helpful when grocery shopping. Reasonably, we all know the temptations that will arise when we take certain foods home. A famous example of using reasonable mind to avoid temptation is in Homer's *Odyssey*, when Odysseus, knowing that when he hears the Sirens he will be too weak to resist steering the ship to pursue them, requests that his men bind him to the mast, allowing him to sail past temptation rather than dashing his ship on the rocks and jeopardizing his voyage home (his long-term goal). Similarly, we can free ourselves up by preparing, using such tools as sticking to a list, not shopping when we are hungry, and choosing planned rewards or treats (rather than impulsive ones).

At times, during or after eating, people feel a sensation of fullness and may conclude they have overeaten or are fat (Fairburn 2008). Any of several events may prompt this conclusion, including a physical sense of fullness; thoughts that you have eaten too much; the feeling of your clothing being tight; or perceiving your abdomen as being distended. It is important to remember that thoughts and feelings are not always factual and that thus it's not true that you are fat just because you think or feel you are. For example, if before the meal you felt fine, and afterward you felt fat, the fact is that it is impossible to gain a substantial amount of weight at one meal. So this feeling of "being fat" can fluctuate independent of changes in your actual weight—the experience of feeling fat is often a product of emotion mind. Also, even if in fact you are overweight, getting caught in emotion mind around *feeling* fat will not move you forward.

Do you ever notice feeling fat? What other thoughts and emotions are occurring when this thought arises? Many people feel fat when they are sad, lonely, or bored. You may also feel fat as a result of comparisons or around such sensations as bloating. It may be helpful to bring awareness to feeling fat; the following exercise is designed to help you do so.

Exercise: Noticing Feeling Fat

Think of a situation where you got caught up in feeling fat, and use the following questions to help bring your awareness to other factors in the situation.

1. What was the situation? (Just the facts: where were you, whom were you with, what events happened, and so forth.)

2. What state of mind were you in? What emotions, comparisons, or perceptions did you experience that might have contributed to your feeling fat?

3. If you were in that situation again, what might you try to attend to the fat feeling and possibly change the way this experience affects you?

♥

Summary

Henry David Thoreau wrote discerningly, "Only that day dawns to which we are awake." That is to say, we can appreciate moments (and morsels) only when we awaken and attend to them.

In this chapter on the concept and practice of mindfulness, we examined the ways emotions, states of mind, and the judgments that flow from them can keep us from experiencing present reality. We saw how emotions and habit can distort the ways we perceive our feelings of hunger and satiety, and we practiced slowing down and paying attention to physiological feelings. We explored how different states of mind can operate in different situations and practiced ways to notice our state of mind and how it affects our decision-making and perspectives around eating and body image. Bringing awareness to whether we are in emotion mind, reasonable mind, or wise mind can help us change not only our behavior but even our feelings about our shape.

Distraction from the present moment is not always and eternally undesirable—there are times you want to distract yourself, like when you are getting a root canal. But living our lives out of habit and routine, driven by unexamined states of mind, means we miss experiences we may relish, whether meals or moments with loved ones. We may fill our bellies with a lot of food and very little awareness or with a lot of awareness and enough food.

Chapter 4

EMOTIONAL INTELLIGENCE

Between stimulus and response there is a space. In that space is our power to choose our response. In our response lies our growth and our freedom.

—VIKTOR E. FRANKL

You're standing in the checkout line in the grocery store. Your shopping cart is full of food. The line is long, your patience is low, and a small child behind you is ramming a cart into your calf. The day has been rough—the weather bad and the traffic awful. Plus, you're hungry and tired and you hate the grocery store. Your phone rings and it's your critical cousin. She's predictably calling to berate you. What do you do?

A. Answer, act polite and apologetic, and erupt inside.

B. Curse at her and hang up.

C. Ignore the call, listen to the message, and dwell on how miserable you feel.

D. Take a deep breath, explain this isn't a good time, and tell her you appreciate her understanding that you're busy.

E. Pick up a chocolate bar and add it to your groceries. Your patience was spent on not yelling at the cart-shoving child's dad, and the call from your cousin was just too much.

Often, choices A, B, and C relate to choice E. When we suppress emotions by acting disingenuously, reacting angrily, or ruminating, emotions can feel overwhelming and we may lose contact with the moment and with our freedom to choose our behavior. In this chapter, we will begin to explore how to sit with emotions with both acceptance and skill.

Understanding Emotions

Emotions may be triggered in many different ways, including changes in your experience, behavior, and physiological response system. Emotions unfold in a particular sequence. *If we understand and accept the building blocks of an emotion, we can change the emotion by changing a part of the process.* In this process, we are both accepting an emotion and moving toward change, when change is useful (Linehan 1993a, 1993b).

Basically, an emotion arises when we experience something (a situation, a memory, a thought); we evaluate it (appraisal); and then we notice changes in our bodies and feel a pull toward taking an action in response to that feeling (Gross and Thompson 2007; Linehan 1993b). We get a rude phone call, think about how bad our day was, have the thought that life's not fair, feel tense and hot and feel a pull to suppress the emotion, yell at someone to release it, or indulge in a sweet treat to ameliorate it. Our thoughts and behaviors affect how we feel, and our feelings affect our thoughts and behaviors.

As discussed in chapter 1, emotions often serve important functions. At times, however, you may feel as though you aren't able to manage certain emotions, and feelings may hurt more than help. This is particularly true when you experience emotions more intensely than is helpful in a situation. For instance, experiencing tremendous anxiety about your eating may actually get in the way of your eating skillfully and increase the likelihood that you will use food to cope.

In this chapter, we'll explore ways to both reduce the *vulnerabilities* that make us more susceptible to intense feelings and manage emotions by changing *situations*, practicing mindful *attention*, noticing *appraisals*, and altering the *response* components of emotions (Linehan 1993b). In the example above, you are more susceptible to feeling agitated by your angry cousin because you've had a bad day and feel hungry and tired. Plus, your history with your cousin and her snide remarks makes you more likely to interpret her comments as an attack. Your appraisal, "Life's not fair," and an avoidant response such as suppressing your feelings while on the phone and buying a chocolate bar, affect the way you experience your sadness. Many of the ideas introduced in this chapter will be expanded on in later chapters. Before we jump into the specifics of changing an emotion you would like to change, we'll explore emotions, and the concept of *emotional intelligence*, more generally.

Emotional Intelligence Equals Awareness and Flexibility

We react to circumstances and events—we're not highly trained, stoic guards at Buckingham Palace! And the fact is we will never be able to experience freedom if we are always running away from our feelings. We will never experience meaning when our chief objective is to not feel bad. Feelings arise, and when we are aware, accepting, and flexible, we are able to respond according to choice, setting a deliberate course rather than rigidly following a narrow path prescribed by our fear of feeling bad. This is the path to freedom and meaning.

In 1995, Daniel Goleman published the best-selling book *Emotional Intelligence*, in which he argues that awareness of one's own emotions and the emotions of others, as well as the ability to manage emotions and impulses, influence the ways we experience our lives. He further argues that these emotion-related abilities are worth considering when we think about the concept of intelligence—that they actually constitute their own kind of intelligence. And, according to Goleman, we can increase our emotional intelligence.

What comes to mind when you consider emotional intelligence? Social psychologists John Mayer and Peter Salovey (1997) define emotional intelligence as the ability to:

1. Accurately perceive emotions in oneself and in others

2. Understand emotions and signals conveyed by emotions

3. Use emotions to enhance thinking

4. Manage emotions to achieve goals

Let's see how these play out in real life.

Pamela's Story

Pamela, a forty-two-year-old, newly divorced photographer, came to therapy to work on understanding her emotions and feeling less overwhelmed by them. She arrived at one of our weekly sessions beaming with pride, saying she'd had a difficult encounter and that she practiced using some of the skills she had worked hard to master. She told me she'd felt slighted when Greg, a new acquaintance whom she had gone out with a few times, canceled their Friday night date at the last minute, saying vaguely he "wasn't feeling great." She was aware of such thoughts as "He doesn't like me" when they arose in her mind, and she was able to not take them as facts. Pamela also noticed her heart began to race and her face tensed when she heard his news. She noticed a pull to revisit previous situations of disappointment in romantic relationships, but instead she returned to her current emotions about the canceled date: uncertainty about how to spend the evening and a fear her fond feelings for Greg were unrequited. Initially, she thought about ordering some Chinese food for comfort, crying, and calling Greg to cancel plans to go watch the football game with him later that week. Her thoughts, in essence, were: "Well, if he canceled on me, I'll show him! I hate football anyhow…"

Instead of acting on these thoughts, however, Pamela sat with her feelings. She realized that deep down she wanted to continue to get to know Greg better and that it would therefore be unhelpful to react impulsively. After all, her deeper values included connecting with people, being kind, and feeling empathic. Pamela also prioritized self-respect, and so she chose to pursue activities on Friday night that mattered to her, including being present with her six-year-old son.

On Saturday morning, Pamela called Greg to see how he felt. Using warmth and a gentle tone, she stated her preference for open communication. Though she sensed his discomfort as she broached the topic, she maintained her warmth rather than pulling away or changing the subject and inquired whether the last-minute cancellation reflected feelings of disinterest. Greg explained he was coming down with a cold and also that he preferred to take things slowly by waiting until they spent more time together before they went out to dinner on a Friday night. Pamela noticed her anxiety growing as a result of the ambiguity, but maintained a sense of openness and interest, which conveyed itself to Greg. She was successfully able to communicate to Greg that she would like to continue to get to know him.

What is emotionally intelligent about all of this? Situations where we feel pain may prompt us to pursue quick fixes involving unhealthy "comfort" foods or impulsive reactions. Pamela, by contrast, was able to sit with her feelings, learn from them, make more mindful choices about how she would proceed, and express herself warmly yet honestly to Greg, increasing her self-respect. She was able to treat herself, her son, and Greg with care and attentiveness.

Primary and Secondary Emotions

In addition to learning to label feelings, it is helpful to notice whether an emotion is primary or secondary. When we experience an emotion that arises automatically, that is a *primary emotion*. *Secondary emotions* are those you experience in response to the primary emotions—feelings about your feelings (Greenberg and Safran 1987; Linehan 1993b). You are in a situation where you feel endangered, so you feel afraid. Fear is primary. Then, you may mull over the feeling, create such judgments as "It's weak to feel afraid," and end up with secondary emotions of more fear, shame, and self-loathing. That is to say, you were simply afraid, but then you begin to think: "There is something wrong with being afraid. It's humiliating." Now, you've added shame to what started as fear. Here are the equations:

Fear + Acceptance = Fear

Fear + Nonacceptance = Fear, Shame, Self-Loathing, More Fear

Do you ever feel anxious and then feel ashamed about feeling anxious? Depressed about feeling depressed? Sad, and then angry about it? When noticing an emotion, bring particular awareness to whether the emotion is primary or secondary.

One of the ways to bypass an avalanche of secondary emotions is to notice what emotion you experience first and attend to thoughts and feelings about that emotion. By *validating*, or acknowledging how you feel with acceptance, you may be less likely to generate secondary emotions (e.g., Linehan 1993a). Validation includes normalizing your emotion, such as thinking: "It makes sense that I'd feel sad that I didn't get that promotion. It's normal to feel that way." Validation is not to be confused with treating yourself as fragile or validating unskillful behaviors (such as "It makes sense that I yelled; I was really angry," if you are committed to working on your anger).

Invalidating responses include judging or not accepting your emotions. In the supermarket, in the example from earlier in the chapter, if you were to notice that you felt sad, you might acknowledge to yourself, "Given the events of the day, feeling sad makes a lot of sense." Alternatively, you might think, "I'm all worked up about that stupid call. I'm too sensitive and pathetic." What sorts of secondary emotions may follow from such an invalidating response? Probably more sadness and shame will arise.

It may be useful to step back for a moment and think about a time you experienced an intense emotion and spoke to someone about it. Can you think of a time you felt better after sharing? What did the person do or say? Can you think of a time you spoke about your emotions and felt worse? I'd be willing to wager that when you felt better after sharing an emotional experience, it was because another person validated your feelings. When a friend listens with acceptance or normalizes your emotions by saying, "Anyone would feel the way you feel," you feel validated. In contrast, being interrupted or told "You're too sensitive; get over it" leads to feeling invalidated. The same circumstances that make us feel worse when talking to others about our emotions arise within when we invalidate ourselves.

Exercise: Identifying Primary and Secondary Emotions

Think about a situation where you noticed emotions and also noticed having feelings about your feelings.

1. What was the situation? What emotion did you first notice?

2. Do you notice any thoughts or feelings around your emotion?

3. What secondary emotions arose from the thoughts or feelings?

♥

Exercise: Noticing an Emotion and Adding Validation

Either in the same situation you described in the exercise just above, or in a different situation, notice your feelings and practice validating yourself—accepting the way you feel with understanding.

1. Notice an emotion you experienced. Where were you?

2. Now, spend a few moments genuinely validating your experience: "Given _____, it makes good sense I felt _____." To do this, it may be useful to consider either how you might respond to a friend in the same situation or how an understanding friend might respond when you share your feelings.

♥

When you practice self-validation, you provide yourself with a sustainable way to cope with primary emotions and circumvent secondary emotions. When I think about validation, I think about the horse trainer Monty Roberts. He demonstrates beautifully how treating horses with understanding and validation is most helpful in training them. Horse training with whips doesn't compare to the practice of providing validation. So too, with ourselves, treating yourself the way you may treat a loved one helps you manage emotions and live productively.

Emotion Regulation

There you are, home alone again on a Saturday night. You may enjoy yourself, relishing the coziness and quiet. Alternatively, you may find yourself stuck in such judgments as "I'll be alone forever," while your spoon is stuck in the peanut butter. If you feel sad, you may feel pulled to jump into bed and cry yourself to sleep. Or you may notice sadness and urges related to feeling sad, then actually change the way you feel by acting in ways that are opposite to sadness, like blasting some music and dancing or watching a funny film (Linehan 1993b).

Difficulties in managing your emotions may affect your moods and relationships and may lead to problematic behaviors. *Emotion regulation* is the term for processes that influence which emotions you have and when and how you experience those emotions (Linehan 1993a, 1993b; Gross and Thompson 2007). Many people use food to manage emotions or employ such strategies as suppression or avoidance, which may increase the intensity of an emotion. We'll begin to explore a range of choices to regulate emotions in more helpful ways. One of the important steps in regulating an emotion helpfully is noticing and labeling it as you are having it, and considering its function, as discussed in chapter 1.

In the pages ahead we'll address how to reduce vulnerabilities, modify situations, practice mindful awareness, and act opposite—all skills that will allow you to change the way you experience an emotion while it is unfolding. Figure 3, below, illustrates how any of these factors (vulnerabilities, situation, attention, appraisal, or response) can give us the opportunity to change our emotional experience.

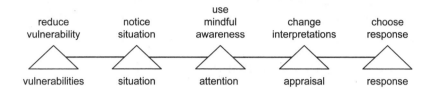

Figure 3: Skills for Changing Emotional Experience

Vulnerability Factors

Our history and recent experiences affect our vulnerability to emotions. Imagine, for example, that you were just insulted by a family member, and then a friend did not return your call. Would you maintain your equanimity? How about if you were in a fabulous mood when your friend did not return your call? *Vulnerability factors* are our emotional states that prime how we may react to a given situation (Linehan 1993b). We are all affected by our temperaments and our histories. We all experience emotions, but we don't all experience them the same way. You may be more prone to experiencing a particular emotion—or all emotions—more intensely than other people you know. Some people describe feeling primed for guilt, while others may not have a particularly sensitive guilt detector. If you tend to experience emotions more intensely than most people, you are *emotionally vulnerable*. Individuals with emotional vulnerability often experience their emotions taking over and may feel powerless to shift their emotional state (Linehan 1993a).

If you have loved ones who are critical of emotions and use food to cope, it makes good sense that you are more vulnerable to using eating to cope when you experience emotions (notice: that was an example of validation!). After all, you have been told (whether implicitly or explicitly), "It is weak to feel and okay to eat." If your father struggled with rage, you may find your own anger scary, and consequently you may try to avoid expressing any anger and instead eat when you feel angry.

In addition to our histories affecting our vulnerabilities, lifestyle habits and recent events can affect our susceptibility to certain feelings. Lack of sleep or too much sleep, insufficient or excessive amounts of food, mind-altering substances (including caffeine), physical illness, and recent relationship chaos all magnify the volume of our feelings (Linehan 1993b).

Starvation or Overeating

Too little food is an emotional and a physical vulnerability for problematic eating. As a DBT therapist, I often receive calls from people struggling with intense emotions. One of the first issues I assess is recent eating behavior. At times, a client has eaten too little or too much in the midst of an emotional crisis. It's hard to tease apart which comes first—does the intense emotion lead to abstaining or indulging, or is an emotion experienced more intensely as a result of insufficient caloric intake or a recent binge? When we don't eat enough, our brains lack enough glucose, and we possess less willpower to make reasonable choices (Baumeister and Tierney 2011). Too much food also affects energy (Zhang et al. 2008), and many people feel sad, irritated, and ashamed after overeating.

Many people try to limit calories after they believe they have eaten too much. This strategy may make sense in the moment as a repair of sorts, but in reality, it creates emotional and physical vulnerability. Experts in the area of binge eating recommend resuming normal eating at the next scheduled meal to avoid a cycle of overeating and restricting. Dieting often leads to preoccupation with food and eating, bringing anxiety, and binges often arise in response to urges that arise from restricting (Fairburn 2008).

Exercise: Awareness of Your Vulnerabilities

Ask yourself the following questions:

1. Which emotions/situations make me vulnerable to eat for emotional reasons?

2. What habits make me more vulnerable to eat for emotional reasons?

♥

There are numerous preventative behaviors that may help you reduce your emotional vulnerability. Of course, you can maintain a healthy sleep schedule, eat the right amount of healthy foods, make sure to eat every few hours so you don't find yourself famished, abstain from mind-altering substances, and seek treatment for any physical illnesses you may have (Linehan 1993b).

You can also increase your awareness around your particular emotional vulnerabilities. Knowing that you tend to get sad if you overeat, and that you eat in response to fatigue, may allow you to pay special attention to sleeping and overeating. In other words, use your awareness of your vulnerabilities to reduce your vulnerabilities.

Another thing you can do is practice validating your feelings. Telling yourself, "Hey, I'm exhausted and just overate; of course I'm feeling sad," may ameliorate and demystify your sadness and can help you sit with the emotion rather than spending time ruminating or beating yourself up for your feelings.

Adding Positive Emotions

Increasing activities that are pleasing to you, both in the short and in the long term, reduces your level of vulnerability. Just as making deposits to your bank account prepares you for financial setbacks, so too deliberately adding positive emotions to your experience can serve as a buffer for experiences that take a toll on you emotionally. Often, people who eat for emotional reasons lack other ways to self-soothe. Purposefully adding pleasant events to your life may reduce your emotional vulnerability, help you learn to manage emotions in other ways, and broaden your focus (Linehan 1993b).

Zindel Segal, the founder of mindfulness-based cognitive therapy, introduced me to a particular way we may assess our vulnerabilities. Take a moment to consider your daily routine, and jot down today's activities and responsibilities. Now, review your daily activities and label each either N for *nourishing*, a task that gives you a sense of vigor or restores you, or D for *depleting*, a required duty that seems to wear you down, physically or emotionally. What is your ratio of nourishing to depleting activities? It may not be realistic to expect to have a perfect 1:1 ratio of nourishing to depleting activities, but if the ratio is weighted much more heavily to depleting activities, adding more nourishing activities can help you feel more engaged in and rejuvenated by your life. Adding nourishing moments such as taking the time to listen to the rain fall or to eat a slow lunch, tasting each bite, can help buffer stress and difficult emotions. In my own life, I've noticed that waking up early to practice yoga, even when my mind is screaming, "Sleep in," and walking slowly to my favorite coffee place mitigates my daily hassles.

Show Up for Pleasant Events

Purposefully adding nourishing activities to your life may reduce your sense of depletion, and participating in pleasant events may actually engender joy. It's good to plan pleasant events: to enjoy them, it's helpful to show up mentally too (Linehan 1993b). When you are mindful, you are participating fully in the experience. Can you think of events you may find pleasing? At times, we may feel so down that it is difficult to predict that anything will actually be fun. It may be worthwhile to consider activities that you may enjoy, and then simply experiment, letting go of judgments or expectations. Wishing something was more enjoyable will make it less pleasant.

Generally, it is helpful to pursue events that are enjoyable both in the short term and in the long term. Planning a day to see a movie is nice. At the same time, it's useful to also schedule events that will reduce vulnerability in the long run, such as keeping in touch with supportive friends.

What sorts of nourishing activities might you enjoy? Many of my clients find volunteering, taking a weekly class, or joining such a group as a book club or shared interest meeting (you might visit www.volunteer match.org or www.meetup.com) helpful in terms of structuring positive events to occur regularly. You may also consider a daily pleasant event such as taking a walk, sitting in the bath, buying flowers for your desk, reading, listening to music, dressing up... Can you think of seven potentially nourishing activities to add to your week? Use the following exercise to keep track of your experience of them.

Exercise: Adding Emotional Nourishment

Schedule several pleasant events. Afterward, if you find it helpful, use this format to organize your observations on these activities in your notebook.

Day	Pleasant activity planned	What I actually did	Mindfulness (0–10)	Enjoyment (0–10)	Observations on how activity affected emotional eating

♥

Create Mastery

In addition to doing things we enjoy, it is helpful to purposefully create opportunities to experience a sense of accomplishment (Linehan 1993b). Persistently creating opportunities to experience a sense of competence will serve as a safeguard against feeling helpless. As a trader, Bruce spent the entire day in front of four computer monitors watching the stock market. He felt underwhelmed, bored, and purposeless. "I did not pursue three advanced degrees to watch the market, lose my mind, and snack," he complained. What is the message in his boredom? Bruce is a person who values challenge and accomplishment. He decided to take a course in Japanese and studied each night, which gave him a sense of accomplishment. He also began to explore karate, where he felt enthusiastic about the prospect of progressing to more advanced belts. Bruce is brutally judgmental, and initially he tended to judge himself harshly during his extracurricular mastery pursuits. But these new activities gave him the opportunity to practice mastering a nonjudgmental stance. While Bruce felt hopeless about the economy and his ability to advance in his work, challenging himself and progressing in other areas diminished his vulnerability to feelings of worthlessness, which had often contributed to his soothing himself in the evenings with high-calorie snacks or food from local take-out restaurants. We will spend more time on mastery in chapter 5.

Cope Ahead

How do we generally prepare for an emotionally charged event? Many of us imagine the worst or worry endlessly, but a technique called *coping ahead* is an effective alternative (Linehan 1993b). Rather than drowning in the nightmare in your mind, why not consider realistic challenges and plan ahead to reduce your vulnerability? I imagine that expecting the worst actually increases your vulnerability.

Imagine picturing a future difficult situation—a Thanksgiving dinner with your family, a run-in with your ex. How does the story your mind creates usually go? Generally, we envision the worst-case scenario. You are anxious about flying, so you picture the plane crashing. Do you ever imagine a more realistic, safe landing? Could you picture going to a family dinner where you anticipate there will be stressful conversation and imagine coping well?

If you know you are going to have trouble sticking to reasonable portions when you attend that upcoming buffet brunch, is it helpful to worry while you look in your closet for your elastic-waist pants? What might be a way to cope well? Research has found that athletes improve their game via mental rehearsal (Atienza, Balaguer, and García-Merita 1998). Similarly, individuals who rehearse being assertive in advance of a particular situation are more capable of asserting themselves (Kazdin 1982). Basically, we use the same area of our brain to imagine doing an activity as we do to actually engage in that activity (Jeannerod and Frank 1999). Why not practice coping well instead of preparing yourself for the worst? You may consider ways to cope ahead with food-related triggers as well as challenging emotional situations. What is one upcoming eating-related event or emotionally charged encounter you are anticipating? How might you cope ahead? We actually improve performance and learn a new set of skills by rehearsing.

Rather than mulling over the infinite possibilities of what may go wrong, consider your part in making things right. In addition to visualizing a scenario going well, you may also plan ahead: realistically anticipate what will likely occur, and visualize the steps you will need to cope well. For example, imagine that you are anticipating that you will feel lonely after your dinner with a friend who is visiting from out of town. As you are finishing your meal the waiter asks you whether you would like to take home your leftovers. In this situation, coping ahead might include the awareness that later you may feel lonely and feel pulled to overeat. *Stimulus control* involves understanding that behavior is prompted by the presence or absence of a stimulus. Leaving your unfinished food on your plate instead of asking for a doggie bag may thus help you lessen the likelihood of eating emotionally. Coping ahead involves seeking awareness of potential obstacles and creating specific plans to help you deal with them.

Exercise: Coping Ahead

For this exercise, take out your notebook and go through the following steps to help strengthen your coping ahead skills.

1. Imagine a situation in which you anticipate experiencing intense negative emotions. Explain what may happen, in a paragraph or so, including the events you believe may lead up to your feelings of discomfort.

2. Write down a plan for ways you might cope ahead to manage your emotions and behaviors. What choices can you make both prior to the event and in the moment to lessen the intensity or discomfort?

For example:

1. Coming home from work on Monday night after seeing my sister. I will feel sad that she is going back to Chicago. It will be relatively early in the evening. I'll be tempted to order unhealthful food because I feel sad and bored.

2. I will make sure to eat regular meals today so I am less vulnerable and I will go to the Overeaters Anonymous meeting in my neighborhood for additional support. I'll buy a magazine that I always enjoy at the corner newsstand. I will plan to cook, which I know will be satiating and will be an opportunity to build mastery: the recipe is somewhat complex. I can visualize coming home, surfing my urges [you will learn more about this in chapter 5], and turning to my magazine or calling a friend.

♥

So far, we've covered ways to reduce the vulnerabilities that may affect the way we experience emotions—these ways include being mindful of our vulnerabilities, adding nourishing activities, and considering ways to build mastery and cope ahead. Now let's move to what we do once we face the situation.

Mindfulness of the Situation

Let's return for a moment to the example we started this chapter with, in which you've had a bad day, but let's back it up a bit. There are a number of points at which you might choose different actions based on acknowledging that you're emotionally vulnerable today. You might decide to wait until tomorrow to go shopping. Or, you may decide you're able to handle shopping, but not talking with your cousin. On seeing her name come up on your phone, you might acknowledge: "I feel sad. This is not a good time to talk to her; I'll call back when I'm in a better place." By making mindful decisions based on what we know of our emotional vulnerabilities, we can face situations when we have the inner resources to deal with them in a positive manner.

We may expose ourselves to situations out of habit rather than based on our inner wisdom or values (for more on values, see chapter 9). For example, if you often find yourself in a restaurant with limited healthy food options—mostly because your friend likes the place—this is a habit that you might decide to modify, perhaps by suggesting another restaurant. If you are deeply dissatisfied with your job or a relationship, you may similarly consider ways to problem solve and mindfully modify the situation.

Mindfulness, here, means letting go of judgments or predictions and focusing on the reality of the situation; noticing your emotions; and bringing awareness to your objective. If you aren't mindful, you may fall into routine or get stuck in thoughts that affect your ability to move forward.

Exercise: Noticing and Modifying a Situation

1. Briefly describe a situation you regularly face that can bring up difficult emotions and urges.

2. If you notice any judgments in your thoughts about the situation, replace them with facts or preferences.

3. Consider several ways to modify the situation.

4. Chose one modification as a first choice, and another as a backup plan.

For example:

1. Staying home on Saturday night makes me feel sad, lonely, and like a loser, so I eat ice cream.

2. Staying home on Saturday night is often a situation where I tend to feel sad and lonely because I'd prefer to go out or be with others. [Notice that the term "loser" is omitted; it is a judgment and an appraisal that makes your emotions more intense.]

3. I can call a friend on Tuesday morning to see if we can see a movie or I can read the book I've been interested in, which would make me feel more productive. I can make sure to have healthy snacks and a single portion of ice cream rather than a pint.

4. I'll call the friend and also think of other activities I may pursue alone.

♥

Mindful Awareness

In addition to modifying our situation, we may practice *mindful awareness* when facing difficult experiences. Mindful awareness includes present-moment awareness and acceptance, and willingness to participate in this moment, just this moment, one moment at a time. If you are spending time with your brother and your relationship with your brother is painful, you can think, "I can't believe I'll be here for another three days," and mentally review the entirety of your painful past history with him. Alternatively, you might bring your attention to the present moment, just this one moment, and adopt a nonjudgmental stance. The moment is difficult enough without reviewing the pain of the past and worrying about the future. Breaking a perceived massive situation into strands of moments, thoughts, and feelings is a powerful tool for changing through acceptance.

Let's see how adding mindful awareness might work in the grocery store scenario. As you stand in line, you might focus on one breath at a time rather than reviewing your daily hassles, judging the situation unpleasant, and incessantly checking your watch. Adding mindful awareness to going to the grocery store may give you a mental vacation from a trying day. If you are mindfully noticing your steps or nonjudgmentally observing details of products on the shelves or of the background music, you are not rehearsing the pain and sadness you've just been experiencing—they lose their power, even if only for a moment (and then another...and another...). Use the following exercise to practice staying present mindfully.

Exercise: Staying in the Moment

1. Consider an upcoming situation that feels overwhelming.

2. How might you break the scenario into moments, one moment at a time?

♥

Mindful awareness also includes noticing and labeling your emotions with acceptance. When we are mindful of our emotions, we may notice that, like waves in the ocean, feelings rise and fall. You will not feel the exact same way you feel now forever, or even an hour from now. Mindful awareness is the antithesis of impulsiveness or reactivity. It gives you choice and space between a situation and your response. You are able to notice tension in your body, or feelings of sadness, and accept these without reaching for the chocolate bar.

Exercise: Mindful Awareness of Emotions

1. Notice your emotion without judging it, suppressing it, or dwelling on it. Gentle labeling helps, either silently or softly spoken ("sadness"; "anxiety").

2. Bring your attention to where you experience the emotion in your body.

3. Remember that you are not your emotion, no matter how intense the emotion may feel.

4. Practice accepting your emotion, one moment at a time— allowing it to intensify or lessen, stay or pass, simply noticing it and its effect on your body.

♥

Noticing Interpretations

Our thoughts and beliefs about an event and our appraisals of it—that is, our *interpretations*—affect how we feel. You may find yourself in the exact same scenario and feeling differently depending on your interpretations. Imagine that your friend Alex has succeeded in losing fifteen pounds. If your interpretation is "I'm proud of Alex," how do you feel? If your interpretation is "Everyone has it easier than I do," how do you feel? Are you mindful of your interpretations? Many people go from an interpretation to a feeling so quickly that it's hard to notice that an interpretation is just that—an interpretation.

Stephen Covey, author of the best-selling book *The 7 Habits of Highly Effective People* (2004), described riding a New York subway and noticing a man and his rambunctious children. As the children yelled, the man appeared oblivious. Given the interpretation that these children are out of control and this parent is irresponsible, how might you feel? Covey felt incensed, as we may imagine ourselves feeling. How could a parent shirk responsibility like that? Eventually, Covey gently approached the man and encouraged him to manage the situation. The man responded, saying that his wife had died an hour ago at the hospital, and he wasn't sure how to manage. Covey's anger melted as his compassion surfaced. If you realized the man had just lost his wife and these children had lost their mother, you might reflect, "These children are having a terribly hard time," and feel empathetic. Same situation, different interpretation.

Exercise: Noticing Interpretations and Replacing Them with Facts

1. Describe a situation.

2. Notice your interpretations.

3. What emotions would each interpretation create?

4. Replace your interpretations with either a new interpretation or just the facts.

5. What emotions do you notice when you sit with your new appraisal?

♥

James Gross, a psychology professor at Stanford and an expert in the field of emotion regulation, has examined the way *reappraisal*, or constructing an interpretation to change a situation's emotional impact, affects well-being. Reappraisal means changing an interpretation, and it is not to be confused with *emotional suppression*, which means trying to manage and conceal an emotion by masking the way you feel.

Gross and John (2003) compared the effects of reappraisal as an emotion regulation strategy to those of suppression. People who engaged in reappraisal of their situations were found to experience greater positive emotions and fewer negative emotions in their lives. Reappraisal requires an active and optimistic attitude. People who suppressed their emotions were less aware of their emotions, less able to repair bad moods, and more likely to view their emotions as unacceptable.

Reappraisal also relates to better interpersonal relationships. In the story earlier in this chapter, Pamela was more present with her son when she reappraised Greg's cancellation. Rather than viewing it as proof that she was unlovable or Greg wasn't interested, she successfully reappraised it as a situation that would allow her to spend quality time with her son.

More generally, reappraisal is more strongly associated with well-being. One reason it's a more effective strategy than suppression has to do with timing. Think about the sequence of an emotion: usually, the point at which we will appraise our emotional experience comes sooner in the unfolding of the emotion than the point at which we will suppress the emotion because it has become too painful. We can affect the way we feel and behave by considering our interpretations even as the emotion begins to unfold. We do this by bringing nonjudgmental attention to our vulnerability factors and our interpretations. We'll more thoroughly address the way thinking affects feeling and how to disengage from attachment to thinking in chapter 6.

Do the Opposite

All emotions make sense. Yet at times, fully expressing our emotions is unhelpful. For instance, you may have perfectly good reasons to feel annoyed with your boss. But you also want to keep your job, which means fully expressing your feelings of annoyance may not be your best course of action. If you would like to regulate an emotion because acting on the feeling does not serve you, or because you feel so intensely that your emotion is getting in the way of acting skillfully, it can be useful to practice opposite action. *Opposite action* means noticing an urge related to an emotion and then doing the opposite (Linehan 1993b). Interestingly, doing the opposite actually changes the way you feel: changing your behavior can change your brain! When you feel fear and act on it (say, you run away from a barking dog), you maintain and exacerbate the fear. When you feel fear and stay with it (say, you approach the small, barking dog), the fear lessens and even dissipates.

Doing the opposite is a skill my clients always report finding both incredibly challenging and remarkably useful. In fact, engaging in new behaviors that are independent of your mood is one of the main ingredients in scientifically supported treatments for depression, anxiety, and marital conflict (e.g., Martell, Dimidjian, and Herman-Dunn 2010; Antony, Craske, and Barlow 2006). When a person is depressed, she wants to self-isolate, sleep, and avoid activities. Doing the opposite of feeling sad by purposely becoming active reduces depression. You will also need to practice mindfulness as you take action. For example, if you feel depressed and do the opposite by calling a friend for coffee, it will be hard to change the way you feel if you can manage to think only depressing thoughts while you're with her ("She's only having coffee with me because she feels sorry for me"). In this case, mindfully continuing to check on your interpretations and reappraise will support your feeling better.

Another example of doing the opposite is around anxiety. Anxiety motivates you to avoid whatever makes you anxious. Yet treatments that are helpful for people who are anxious always include approaching and sitting with what makes them anxious. In marriages, when people begin to experience conflict, they move away from acting lovingly. Acting in a loving way, the opposite of indifference, actually increases loving feelings. When I'm listening to a lecture and I notice I feel bored, I've practiced sitting up close to the lecturer, acting interested, and asking thoughtful questions; I then find myself feeling genuinely interested.

Notice that these examples describe situations in which acting opposite to the emotion makes sense. If an emotional urge serves an adaptive function, I would not prescribe doing the opposite. Feeling sad after a loss, running during a robbery, and distancing yourself from a partner who is hurtful are functional behaviors, and those are not times to practice doing the opposite. However, if you are so afraid during a robbery you can't run because you aren't breathing, some amount of doing the opposite of what you feel—for example, slowing down for a moment and breathing—makes sense. *Choose when to do the opposite after mindfully considering whether the action related to your emotion is effective.*

If you feel shame though you haven't done anything that compromises your values, you may act opposite to shame. The first step in doing so would be really noticing shame and what actions it pulls you toward. Shame often makes us want to lower our head, avoid eye contact, and criticize ourselves harshly. Doing the opposite of shame might include standing straight with your head held high, making eye contact, and forgiving yourself. When you love someone who is not reciprocating, or who is not a person you can love given your values, you may choose to do the opposite of love. Love pulls us toward investing time and energy in a person, connecting with, talking about, and thinking about that person. Doing the opposite may include keeping away from the person and moving away from thoughts about him or her. If your general habit is to avoid or eat when emotions are intense, doing the opposite would involve sitting with your feelings and taking special care to eat mindfully (Linehan 1993b).

If your annoyance stems from your boss not giving you a bonus, your interpretation may be that you are not appreciated and you may experience significant anger. Opposite action, including releasing tightness in your jaw, letting go of angry thoughts, and acting kindly toward her, may change the way you feel (and this does not prohibit you from eventually discussing the matter with her). If the fact is that you are unappreciated, showing appropriate disappointment may be useful. However, if your anger is off the charts in magnitude, and fully expressing your anger will lead to your losing your job or jeopardizing your relationship with the person you need as a reference, doing the opposite may be useful.

We've reviewed examples of doing the opposite of fear, sadness, love, shame, and anger. Can you think of a way to do the opposite in your life to change your emotional experience? You may use the following exercise to plan ahead for an upcoming situation, review a previous situation and how you could have acted opposite in retrospect, or practice acting opposite now.

Exercise: Doing the Opposite, Step by Step

1. Notice and label your emotion and pay attention to the actions your emotion is pulling you toward. How intense is the emotion on a scale of 1 to 10?

2. Decide whether acting on the full intensity of your emotion would be harmful or not in your best interest.

3. Do the opposite of your emotion urge, all the way, with your face, body, and thoughts. What does this look like? Describe the choices you make.

4. What do you notice about your emotions after doing the opposite?

♥

Emotional eating is often an action consistent with an emotion (Safer, Telch, and Chen 2009)—not with doing the opposite. As noted earlier in this section, the way you act affects the way you feel. If you feel an emotion and the way you experience it includes eating, eating adds to that emotional experience just as running exacerbates fear. Given this idea, it makes good sense that emotional eating may not really help you change the way you feel. It may be similar to lying in bed when you feel sad. It's part of your behavioral repertoire when you feel a certain way. Overeating when you're sad may be a response consistent with sadness; eating when you're angry may be part of being angry; eating in particular ways when you feel guilty may be a way to punish yourself. When eating is not related to acting on a particular emotion, food may serve as a means to avoid an emotion and thus prolong it rather than changing it. Doing the opposite—meaning not using food to cope with an emotion—is a powerful alternative.

One way to do the opposite and change the way we feel is to change our facial expression of emotion. Our faces naturally change when we experience an emotion. According to the *facial feedback hypothesis*, facial movements influence how we feel. In a fascinating neuroimaging study, participants imitated facial expressions before and after receiving Botox injections in the muscle used in frowning. During their imitation of angry facial expressions, Botox decreased the activation of brain regions implicated in emotional processing and emotional experience in the amygdala and brain stem, compared to activations before the Botox injection (Hennenlotter et al. 2008). These findings show that facial expression modulates emotional processing. You may actually change how you feel by relaxing your facial expression. It is helpful to express difficult emotions in order to garner support from those around you as well as to indicate concern. Still, if the intensity of the emotion is not helpful and you would like to change the way you feel, it may be worth looking at your expression and gently adopting a more relaxed face.

Half-smiling is a specific technique for managing emotions and embodying acceptance (Linehan 1993b). A half-smile entails relaxing your forehead and jaw and ever so slightly raising the corners of your mouth. If you experience any tension, you are not doing it correctly. Consider a pouty expression or a fake smile: both entail facial tension. A half-smile is not intended to be phony. To half-smile, adopt an expression of relaxed acceptance, releasing any facial tension and not forcing a big, toothy grin. After all, if you feel unhappy about your appearance, clenching your teeth and furrowing your brow while looking in the mirror will only fuel sad emotions. Relaxing your expression may help alleviate your discomfort.

Exercise: Mindfully Half-Smiling While Walking

One way to practice mindfulness is to walk mindfully. In this exercise, you may bring attention to the practice of willingness and acceptance as you walk. You may choose to practice this exercise on a walk you typically associate with tension, such as walking to work, running errands, or going to medical appointments.

1. Go for a walk. You may choose to walk somewhere scenic or somewhere routine; the walk may be short or long, whatever you choose.

2. Begin to bring attention to the fact that you are walking. Bring attention to the sequence of actions involved in each step: shifting your weight, lifting your foot, and placing it on the ground.

3. Notice any sensations in your shoulders, and roll your shoulders back to walk in a dignified, upright manner.

4. Next, bring your awareness to your face.

5. Notice any tension in your forehead, eyes, eyebrows, or jaw.

6. Release any tension in your face.

7. Ever so slightly raise the corners of your mouth so that your face adopts an expression of willingness and acceptance as you walk.

8. Notice your breath as you inhale and exhale while maintaining a half-smile.

9. Shift your attention from your body and feet or your breath, to sights and sounds as you walk.

10. When you notice that you have moved away from the half-smile or from a state of present, accepting awareness while walking, that is okay. It is an opportunity to begin again, returning to accepting with your body and your mind.

♥

Half-smiling is a way to act opposite in difficult situations. You may experiment with bringing to mind a person you dislike while half-smiling. You may notice differences in your feelings as you sit with the person, before you or in your mind, while assuming an expression of acceptance.

When you suppress an emotion, you are restraining the feeling and not practicing acceptance. When you change an emotional expression, you are accepting your emotion, relaxing your body, and modifying your experience and expression of the emotion. There's a difference between the two strategies, and it has to do with acceptance. Acting opposite is not faking; rather it's noticing urges to act in a certain way, then deliberately choosing to change your thoughts and behavior, all with a quality of acceptance. Half-smiling is not insincere; it's noticing when your face conveys nonacceptance and changing your expression to a more accepting one. Imagine when someone asks you to smile for a photograph. I'd bet your face feels quite tense and uncomfortable, especially if you hold it for a while. Try that for a moment if you will: adopt a big, toothy, inauthentic camera smile. When you release the face, take a few moments to let go of any tension you may experience in your face. Then, deliberately release any tension in your forehead, bring your attention to this moment, and ever so slightly raise the corners of your mouth. Notice the difference?

Changing your emotional response is a commitment to engage in a behavior that relates to what matters. Avoiding or suppressing is committing to trying to feel less. The distinction is subtle. For example, if you feel anxious at a party, you may accept your anxiety and choose to act opposite by lifting your head up, making eye contact, introducing yourself, and half-smiling, even if a thought arises that makes you anxious and you don't feel perfectly comfortable. Suppressing is going to the party and trying to look cool and calm. Acting opposite may actually increase your anxiety initially, though over time, opposite action will change the way you feel.

Exercise: Bringing It All Together

Consider an emotion you experienced or anticipate experiencing and consider ways to use some emotion regulation skills to identify and reduce your vulnerabilities, modify the situation if necessary, practice mindful awareness, change your interpretations, and act opposite.

1. What is the emotion, and in what situation did you (or will you) experience it?

2. Notice your vulnerabilities: what are (were) they? What are some ways to reduce these vulnerabilities?

3. Would it be helpful to be mindful of the situation? How might you cope ahead or problem solve?

4. How might you practice mindful awareness around your emotion and the situation?

5. What are (were) your interpretations? Is there another way to think about your interpretations or, in other words, to reappraise them?

6. What is (was) your response? What urges does (did) this emotion pull you toward? Would doing the opposite be appropriate? How might you do the opposite?

♥

Summary

In this chapter, you read about practicing emotional intelligence skills to manage emotions more flexibly. You considered how primary and secondary emotions differ from one another and saw there is a range of options to choose from to affect how you feel. Learning to regulate your emotions will help you choose other ways to cope with feelings besides eating. More importantly, learning to manage emotions will improve your relationships with others and with yourself. Emotional intelligence allows for intelligent living.

Chapter 5

SURFING URGES AND DEVELOPING REALISTIC CONFIDENCE

To stay with that shakiness—to stay with a broken heart,
with a rumbling stomach, with the feeling of hopelessness
and wanting to get revenge—that is the path of true
awakening.

—PEMA CHÖDRÖN

D o you find that the more you crave, the more you cave? There you are, patiently standing in line for coffee. You see a fresh cranberry muffin and begin to ponder: "If I don't buy it, I won't stop thinking of cranberry muffins all morning. I had breakfast, but I still feel hungry. Probably because I didn't sleep that well. In fact, I *need* some sugar to boost my energy. Anyway, it's not worth starting the day disappointed when I kind of loathe my job." Soon your mouth is full of cranberry muffin.

Urges may be physical, psychological, or some combination of the two. The muffin scenario is both. And once our emotions are involved, they may affect both our physiology and our appetite. Have you noticed anxiety leading to an experience of shakiness that you perceive as hunger? It may be worthwhile to slow down, step back, and consider your current emotions—and whether satisfying a momentary urge (however strong) relates to what you value—*to what you want your life to really be about.* Of course, if you are physically hungry, valuing your health translates to eating healthfully. On the other hand, if you feel sad but also care about learning to cope with negative emotions meaningfully, it may be worthwhile to observe the "hungry" urges and what they really indicate. Are you trying to manage unpleasant feelings by munching them down? Will this approach work in the long term, or even in the short term (after the food has gone down the hatch and regret sets in)?

What Goes Up Must Come Down

In our minds, a greater urge equals a greater need to indulge. This is an *illusory correlation*. An example: even if you noticed that all your acquaintances who are five foot eight wear glasses, it would be inaccurate to assume that height and impaired vision were related. Similarly, just because you have a strong urge for a candy bar, this does not mean that your need for one is any stronger than normal. What would happen if an urge got stronger and stronger and you just noticed it, without reacting? An old college friend of mine smoked several packs of cigarettes a day. His family lived in Singapore, and flights between New York City and Singapore are eighteen hours long—or, in his terms, thirty cigarettes' worth of time! When asked how he managed his cravings on the long smoke-free flights when he visited his family, he explained, "They get real bad, and they pass, and they get bad, and they pass." In being forced to endure his urges without acting on them, my friend (though unwillingly) experienced the fundamental principle of urges: they swing up and they swing down.

The fact is that often, we simply forget our cravings (and we also forget this fact!). Have you had urges that simply escape your memory? Take a minute to think about urges you experienced yesterday. You may have had urges to say something, indulge in a sweet treat, or snooze. What happened to these urges?

There are also urges we escape due to circumstances. Can you bring to mind an urge that you experienced intensely that you did not satisfy?

You so badly craved lemon sorbet; your mouth watered. When you got to the gourmet shop, you found that that zesty palate cleanser was sold out. What happened next? Chances are, you felt a twinge of disappointment and drove home. Lemon sorbet lost its luster for the time being.

By contrast, what happens when we indulge a craving? The more we give in to our urges, the more we crave and the weaker our ability to resist. To put it simply, *consequences influence behavior*. The more we indulge in a habit, the more habitual it becomes. Ever work in an office with a candy jar? It may be more manageable to never stick your hand in the candy jar, instead of reaching for a gummy bear on your way to the copy machine—otherwise, before you know it, it's as though eating a gummy bear is part of the copying process. Have you ever had one gummy bear and felt satisfied? (Note that this is possible with mindful eating.) Now add stress to the equation. You feel stressed, and there are gummy bears to console you. Eating gummy bears becomes part of the stress loop. You feel stressed, you eat gummy bears, you feel stressed as well as bad about the gummy bears, you feel more stressed, and you eat more gummy bears.

It's important to notice that indulging food urges is reinforcing on multiple levels. Laurie, a thirty-four-year-old woman, loathed her work as an attorney and often brooded anxiously about other potential careers that would afford her the opportunity to pay off her Ivy League loans. In the meantime, she was understandably reticent to complain and was diligent in her work at a prominent law firm. Before major deadlines, Laurie worked fifteen-hour days, and her expression of stress and anxiety was apparent to all who passed the glass walls of her office. Her shoulders slumped and her face tensed. Her paralegal, Jack, knew Laurie's tastes in comfort food. When he noticed her head fall into a pile of papers on her desk, he stepped out to buy her the delicacies she seldom ate on her low-carbohydrate diet: gnocchi, biscotti, and a mocha latte. Laurie looked euphoric as Jack approached with her treats. She also felt indebted to Jack and obligated to enjoy them. Her appreciation was contagious, and Jack was grateful for her warmth.

Notice, there are several layers of reward here. First, there is a *positive reinforcement* to eat. In other words, eating adds something pleasing to the situation. Food is reinforced internally and socially. Laurie enjoys eating her "forbidden" foods as a treat, and she also enjoys pleasing Jack by showing her enthusiasm. How often have we pleased our grandmothers by eating their chicken soup? In addition, there is also a *negative reinforcement* attached to eating here; that is, it is pleasing because it removes a negative state. Laurie's impromptu feast means that she gets a break from the legal nightmare and its emotional effects. As we can observe, eating for emotional reasons is rewarding on a couple of levels.

Now that we understand the benefits in emotional eating, let's better understand some of the consequences. While the food is delicious and temporarily energizing, when she uses it, Laurie fails to learn other ways to cope with emotions. Also, soon enough, perhaps mid-bite, Laurie begins to feel guilty and anxious about loading up on empty calories and carbs, leaving her not only stressed and anxious about work, but stressed and anxious (and guilty) about eating unhealthfully.

In summary:

1. Stopping emotion X by eating leads you to mistakenly believe you cannot otherwise manage X.

2. Managing emotions through food may create secondary negative emotions.

3. The more frequently you use food to manage emotions, the more ingrained this habit becomes.

The brain is active and plastic. We strengthen neural connections underlying our behaviors when we engage in repeated actions. In contrast, refocusing and changing behaviors alters the brain. Rebuilding neural pathways is a process. The good news is that over time, the link between the behavior and engaging in the urge will be weakened. Jeffrey M. Schwartz, a renowned psychiatrist at the University of California–Los Angeles, is well known for his work in treating obsessive-compulsive disorder (OCD). While you may not suffer from OCD, if you can understand the way behavior changes one's brain, you will learn something important about coping with your urges.

People with OCD struggle with intrusive, anxious thoughts and may engage in habits, such as checking or hand-washing, to reduce their anxiety. Schwartz developed an effective treatment for OCD as well as other problematic habits. He noticed three main differences in brain scans between individuals with OCD and those without it. The *orbital frontal cortex*, part of the frontal lobe, fires in awareness of mistakes and is more active in an obsessive person. The *cingulate gyrus* emotes a "mistake feeling," causing an experience of panic, which is also heightened in OCD. Lastly, the *caudate nucleus* allows our minds to shift focus, but in OCD, the caudate nucleus seems to get stuck, causing a lack of mental flexibility (Schwartz and Beyette 1996). In other words, a person suffering from OCD becomes "caught" in intense feelings of making a mistake, in physical symptoms of anxiety, and in difficulty shifting attention. These changes are apparent in neuroimaging studies. Schwartz's treatment changes brain circuits by modifying the neurological links involved. He encourages patients to "manually" (that is, deliberately) shift attention and focus fully on another (pleasurable) activity when urges arise. First, patients are taught to label their experience, so rather than thinking for example "Germs!" and feeling "fear, panic, anxiety!" they reinterpret these thoughts and feelings as "OCD." This act of relabeling creates some perspective. Next, the patient is taught to refocus in the moment and deliberately engage in a pleasant activity.

In this therapy, the *doing* is more important than the feeling. How does this work given our discussion of reinforcement? Not engaging in the urge weakens the reinforcing principle of an urge, while engaging in a new behavior becomes reinforcing in itself. Simply put, this process leads to the creation of new brain circuits, which compete with the existing ones. When Schwartz examined patients after such treatment, the three areas of the brain that were previously "locked," or inflexible, had begun to fire in a normal way.

Brain scans similarly illustrate that emotional eaters and nonemotional eaters differ in their caudate nucleus response when presented with a chocolate shake or other temptation. This suggests that emotional eaters may be more sensitive to some of the rewards of food. Also, emotional eating relates to increases in expectation of enjoying food, as well as increases in the pleasure of eating while in a negative mood (Bohon, Stice, and Spoor 2009). These multiple rewards make sense given what we know about the complexity of emotional eating. Food can be reinforcing on multiple levels, giving immediate pleasure as well as relieving emotional pain. However, Schwartz's research points to the possibility of changing neural pathways. If Laurie (our ambivalent and overfed attorney) were to stop, observe the force of her emotions, and then—instead of eating—deliberately relax her shoulders, release her facial tension, slow her breathing, and listen to her favorite music, she may, over time, similarly change her obsessive habit. (She'll have to have a gentle talk with Jack, too.)

Urge surfing, a term coined by G. Alan Marlatt, director of the Addictive Behaviors Research Center at the University of Washington, describes a technique to observe the rise and fall of a craving. In 1985, Marlatt established the concept of urge surfing to help individuals who struggled with substance abuse. Urge surfing has since been generalized to help people who struggle with food cravings, preoccupations, and binges. The metaphor of surfing is wonderfully apt. Just as ocean waves rise and fall, our urges wax and wane, as do our emotions. Even the tallest wave must subside. Skilled surfers ride above waves and maintain balance in every circumstance. They demonstrate a fluidity and artful flexibility that may be described as dancing on water. (I like the image of water dancing, which speaks to the complexity as well as the adventure involved in the activity.) Kelly Slater, the nine-time world champion surfer, advises that surfing requires knowing the water and which waves to ride, maintaining balance, and embracing failure. Why not, then, view an urge as a refreshing ripple to appreciate rather than a problem to be solved?

Living and Longing

There is no way to completely extinguish desires, and often the attempt to do so creates more suffering. To surf urges, cravings, or preoccupations with food, you must let go of judgment. Wishing you did not think about jelly donuts will not make them (or the wishes) disappear. In fact, being unwilling and negativistic is a recipe for becoming stuck.

Blair's Story

Blair struggled with binge eating and obesity. She worked diligently to avoid "triggers" by eating only at health food restaurants and seldom dining with other people. However, in New York City, there is food everywhere. Blair angrily panicked when faced with food carts, pretzel stands, ice cream trucks, and a city full of people eating on the go. "In a country full of obesity, there should be no food trucks!" she raged. When Blair encountered an ice cream truck on the first day of summer (after rigorously abstaining from stumbling upon "binge foods") she became negativistic, believing it was "unfair"; she felt she could not cope, and she "knew" that if she did not satisfy her urge she would feel worse. Often, her binge eating occurred while she was walking. She would notice the food truck, feel anxious and depressed by her weight, and sense her urges mount. Blair wrongly believed that abstaining would lead to a long-standing sense of deprivation and would exacerbate her depression. Learning to notice her emotions as well as the transience of her urges was instrumental in Blair's letting go of bingeing. She began to consider as she walked: "How long does an urge actually last? Can I actually regulate food truck locations? This may be a moment to practice acceptance and self-compassion." The combination of reminding herself that urges pass and expanding her awareness by paying attention to her feet on the ground, her breath, the architecture of buildings, and the people around her cured her myopic focus on the food truck parade.

Indulging Your Urge

While it is futile to judge urges as "good" or "bad," it is worthwhile to determine whether acting on an urge is helpful or not. Urge surfing requires mindfulness, the ability to be present and observe. We have urges all day long. An urge for chocolate does not necessarily have to afford you the opportunity to urge surf. If you wish, you can enjoy the chocolate and use your urge as an opportunity to be mindful of the pleasant sensations that go along with eating something that tastes good. The key is to make the decision with intention, rather than indulging mindlessly or out of a feeling of defeat. Use your judgment to follow a middle path where you savor enjoyable foods in moderation. One way to determine whether a behavior is helpful is to consider how you will feel not only the moment you indulge, but also over time. For example, enjoying a slice of your father's eightieth birthday cake may be something you remember fondly.

Urge Surfing vs. Willpower

Many people subscribe to the myth that the ability to resist an urge is a limited resource, like an energy supply—hence the term "willpower." What are your thoughts? If you resist an urge now, are you less able to resist later? In a DBT group I run, I encouraged participants to practice mindfully urge surfing in the room by noticing the rise and fall of urges to move around. One participant commented after the practice, "I have enough *real* urges I have to stomach all the time, so why should I use my energy on one that doesn't really matter?" This is a brilliant question that begs another question: is there a particular amount of urge resistance we all have that gets used up? In movies, this "limited supply" of resistance is often depicted. The married female lead has been attracted to her gardener for two years, and finally, she can no longer suppress her desire and begins an extramarital affair. In a commercial, a person tries to stick to her diet, but after a while, the chips look so damn good, it's impossible.

Experimentally, too, self-control has been shown to be a limited resource. If you exert control in one paradigm, you may have less ability in a situation shortly after. In a study by Mark Muraven, Dianne Tice, and Roy Baumeister (1998), asking participants to regulate their emotional responses to an upsetting movie led to decreases in physical stamina. Similarly, if you are in a negative emotional state, managing your mood depletes you of energy and you may have less self-control as a result. As you may know, dieters are more likely to break their diets if they are experiencing a negative mood (e.g., Greeno and Wing, 1994). Practicing mindfulness and acceptance of urges is quite different from trying to fight or suppress urges, as people often do when trying to exercise self-control. We have more energy and less emotional suffering when we accept urges. Additionally, urge surfing may be helpful in minimizing the amount of self-control you anticipate you need. Knowing that an urge will pass keeps you from becoming caught. You may be mindful of your emotional state and soothe yourself in other ways—until your metaphorical self-control power supply is replenished.

Urges and Emotions

You may be wondering, if difficult emotions are linked to urges, how will you manage urges if you keep struggling with difficult emotions? Emotions, like urges, rise and fall. I was raised by my beloved grandma, and for most of my life, my greatest fear was her death. I vividly remember losing her: As I stood in the waiting area of the hospital, I felt sad, hopeless, anxious, and every other negative emotion. I actually began to believe I would never be able to move. I had the thought I might never be able to see a client again because of my pain. I was miserable. And my misery ebbed and flowed. While I still feel twinges of pain when I think of my grandmother, these are now linked to a softer sense of gratitude that I had her in my life.

Urge Surfing Step by Step

When you are in the midst of struggling with an urge, here are some things you can do to decrease your discomfort.

1. Slow down your mind and body. We often act on automatic pilot, and slowing down can help us notice our thoughts and feelings and make mindful choices about them.

2. Let go. Nonjudgmentally observe the urge. Where do you sense it in your body? What is your mind telling you? If you could rate the urge on a scale of 1 to 10 in terms of intensity, where is it now?

3. Refocus. Where are you? What are you feeling? In the long term, how will you feel if you indulge the urge? How will you feel in the long term if you surf the urge?

4. Choose. After you make space for the urge and let go of judging, you have some room to decide. Where is the urge now? Is it slowly mounting? Are you willing to watch it rise? If not, can you practice letting the discomfort exist for just a little while longer than you might otherwise, before you give in to it?

As always, be dubious of anything I suggest until you have experimented and found the practice helpful. Would you be willing to try urge surfing? The following exercise is designed to give you some experience of it. After the practice, you may generate some ideas of situations in which you tend to notice urges to eat for emotional reasons, and then experiment with urge surfing in those moments.

Exercise: Urge Surfing

1. Focus on an urge you have right now, such as shifting in your chair, logging on to your favorite social networking website, letting your mind wander, or scratching your back.

2. Sit with that urge for a few minutes, observing it without acting on it.

3. Try describing the urge, either in your head or by writing it down. What does it feel like? Where do you feel it in your body? What is your mind telling you about the urge? On a scale of 1 to 10, with 10 being extremely uncomfortable, how would you rate the urge right now?

4. Sit with the urge for another minute, and then rate it again. Has the level of discomfort changed?

5. Practice not giving in to the urge for as long as you are able. How long were you able to do it? How did the urge change or shift as you paid attention to it? Did you finally give in? How did that feel? If you didn't give in, how did that feel? Observe your reactions without judgment.

   Do this exercise any time you want to practice your urge surfing.

   ♥

Aikido is a Japanese art of self-defense in which you blend the motion of the attacker and the redirected force of the attack, rather than confronting it head on. This requires mental as well as physical strength.

Relaxation and flexibility are fundamental. Similarly, you may garner the most strength by flexibly relaxing, accepting, and rolling with what comes your way. Weave and surf; don't throw punches. With practice, you will be able to maintain your balance throughout the inevitable onslaught of life and its resultant urges. Remember, new neural pathways are not created in an instant! But if you can master this mental aikido of urge surfing, you can stare down any cranberry muffin.

Developing Realistic Confidence

Urge surfing isn't easy. However, building *realistic* confidence may increase your sense that you can in fact cope with urges. If we consider confidence a general attitude, developing skills in a broad range of areas in your life may boost your self-assurance when you're facing urges. Plus, accomplishing goals improves your mood. You may struggle with urges for particular foods, urges to instantly gratify yourself by avoiding feelings, and urges to quit your plans to practice mindfulness. Through deliberate attempts to pursue activities that require effort, you can chip away at beliefs you hold about yourself and what you can and can't do.

Now! Drum roll, please, for the question every motivation-eliciting pep talk includes: what is the difference between those who succeed in accomplishing a goal, such as urge surfing, and those who do not? I don't want to presume I have *the* answer to this complex question. So let's slow down and wonder together: What thwarts action? What would potential remedies include?

Imagine that one of your long-standing goals is to run a marathon, twenty-six miles. What steps are necessary to get to the physical fitness level you need to achieve before you can run a marathon? According to Olympic athlete and running coach Jeff Galloway, to prep for the marathon, you begin by running or walking for thirty minutes, twice a week, and you methodically build your endurance over time. In twenty-nine weeks, you can go from being unable to run more than three miles to running twenty-six miles. This is not a late-night infomercial; this is a program thousands of people like you and me have followed to make marathon running a realistic ambition. In order to build a sense of realistic confidence in a goal, then, break a task into manageable chunks. *To develop a sense of confidence more generally, regularly challenge yourself.*

We are all faced with challenges. *Mastery* means doing things that make you feel competent and confident (e.g., Linehan 1993b). *Self-efficacy,* or your beliefs about your ability, has a major impact on your life. You build your sense of self-efficacy through mastery. Some people wait until they feel confident to begin a challenge. What is the alternative? *Build competence by deliberately identifying goals that are both difficult and possible.* Ask yourself, "Where is my goal on the continuum from effortless to unattainable?" Mastery is all about being in the middle of that spectrum.

Almost any effective program in which you change an existing behavior includes some reasonable step to engender hope to take the next. Think about Alcoholics Anonymous, whose motto is "One day at a time," not "Don't drink for the rest of your life." Chances are the latter sentiment would breed anxiety and thus perhaps lead to drinking, while the former seems manageable and increases the chances of abstinence. A patient of mine once described developing mastery as "tricking the brain" by circumventing paths that lead to resistance. I see taking workable steps as the only way to build optimism, adequately preparing you for change in the relationship between your emotions and food.

Mastery and Urge Surfing

Urge surfing requires a sense of mastery, and surfing urges builds mastery. Knowing you have trained enough that you can run a marathon provides a base of realistic confidence in other areas: "Of course I can ride the urge to order nachos; I've ridden many urges to quit running!" Similarly, repeatedly surfing the urge to order nachos may also establish both a general sense of self-confidence and the confidence that you can resist the next food pitfall.

When your mind sends you the message "Give up! Why bother?" you can thank your mind for that thought. Thanking your mind for a thought is observing the thought without judgment, rather than responding to the thought as though it is a factual alarm. Then, you can cheer yourself on by reminding yourself of difficult urges you've experienced and surfed. Similarly, practicing urge surfing builds mastery. By repeatedly noticing, labeling, and riding urges, you will build your sense of confidence in your ability to give yourself more space between urge and action.

You may be wondering, "This is a book on emotional eating—why are we addressing mastery in areas other than eating?" Many people who struggle with eating problems make eating the focus of living. Yet it is often helpful to focus on living more broadly so that eating becomes a part of living rather than the focus of living (we will address this more in chapter 9). You may feel like you've worked really hard to abstain from emotional eating. Perhaps stepping back and noticing how you excel in other areas will engender renewed realistic confidence that you can end your emotional eating. We have little incentive to pursue goals if we don't have a sense we will accomplish them.

Building mastery in various areas of your life may reduce your vulnerability to intense emotions and urges. Let's say your desire to offer the wittiest toast at your brother's wedding is creating a lot of stress. Taking a course on public speaking with the goal of mastering your public speaking skills and conquering your fear may reduce the anxiety you experience. In addition, when you problem solve and take steps to build your confidence, you may be less likely to turn to food to cope with your nerves about the speech. And knowing you can sit with discomfort (for example, surfing the urge to feign laryngitis to avoid giving the toast) may spill over and influence your sense of mastery to sit with the urge to eat.

The hopelessness that may arise when we're faced with the arduous task of changing must be replaced by a growing sense of accomplishment. Purposefully engaging in activities to build mastery is a key ingredient in cognitive behavioral therapy for depression, a treatment that has been found to be as effective as antidepressants. When you are depressed, you may experience negative beliefs about yourself, your future, and the world. The experience of accomplishing a relatively challenging goal both challenges negative beliefs and engenders realistic hope. Some people wait until an opportunity presents itself to pursue an activity or socialize. Developing mastery is about purposefully scheduling activities that engender a sense of confidence.

Carol Dweck (2006), a psychology professor at Stanford University, has been studying motivation and achievement for almost forty years. She determined that our *self-theories*—what we believe about what we can achieve—affect what we set out to accomplish. The good news is that you can change your self-theories. Dweck explains that people may have either *fixed mindsets* or *growth mindsets*. This means that you may see yourself as either a lost cause or a work in progress. Mastery begins with a state of mind. I believe that developing mastery in one area may affect your overall self-theory. Would refining your artistic prowess by taking a watercolor class improve your feelings about your ability to manage emotions and food? Chances are, when you notice that your ability to paint improves with practice, you may develop a more growth-oriented mindset in other areas as well.

Pain with a Purpose

Building mastery muscles requires resistance training. Let's be frank. Running to increase your mileage each week is (literally) no walk in the park. Instant gratification is not the game here (nor will it take you far). Mastery, by definition, will not be instantaneous.

In the short term, mastery requires perseverance. In the long run, mastery will improve your mood and reduce your vulnerability to negative emotions. Over time, engaging in challenging actions purposefully will improve self-esteem and reduce feelings of depression. These behaviors give feedback to your brain, rewiring it and dismantling previously held beliefs. People often describe feeling more joy from accomplishment than from seeking instant pleasure. You may be struggling with low self-esteem, questioning your ability to experience a sense of accomplishment, and eating to manage your nerves. As discussed earlier in this chapter, *you may change your brain by modifying your behaviors.* That is, you may change the way you *feel* by *doing.* When thoughts attempt to convince you not to bother with surfing your urges, dealing with your emotions differently, or improving your musical abilities, notice those thoughts—and let them go by like so much background noise. By changing your actual behaviors, you will get unstuck. Eventually, the raucous dissonance in your mind may begin to quiet. Ultimately, you run the marathon with your legs and not your thoughts. It would be nice if your mind helped you along the way, but it is not required. Would you be willing to move your body toward what matters deeply and bring your attention there?

Individuals may travel to a Zen ashram to develop spiritually. They meditate. They also sweep floors. You spend money, travel to a hillside, sit in silence, and scrub toilets. A couple of years ago, I had the opportunity to participate in a meditation retreat with Marsha Linehan, the psychologist who created DBT, in Tucson, Arizona. I envisioned relaxing in the sun, savoring the vegetarian meals, cultivating mindfulness, and becoming a more patient person in a mere five days. I did not expect a 5:30 a.m. wake-up, sitting for six hours a day facing a white wall, and sweeping. All these tasks required mental mastery. After a day of staring at the wall, I broke the practice of silence and asked Marsha if it would be possible to sit outside facing the cacti. She said something along the lines of "Life is about what happens when you're faced with white walls." Anticipating only pleasure, or at least pain-free steps toward growth, may hinder our progress. Thus, the chores we face along the way may be therapeutic. Room service and a concierge will not change your mood in the same way accomplishments change your experience and your sense of self.

The Motivation Myth

"You cannot urge surf or train for the marathon until you are motivated." That statement is a common myth. Motivation is like winning the lottery; it is tenuous and is no guarantee for an enriching life. You are probably thinking you know yourself and you work only when motivated. Do you go to work or do your laundry? Do you feel motivated to do those tasks on a regular basis? Often, even when we experience a surge of motivation, the inspiration is fleeting. Waiting to feel different than you do will mean waiting a long time. Deliberately acting, again and again, will lead to mastery.

Let's get this straight:

1. Motivation is not a prerequisite for action.

2. Action leads to action.

3. Motivation would be nice.

Exercise: Developing Mastery Step by Step

1. Plan to do at least one thing each day to build a sense of accomplishment. You may practice meditation, take a new dance class, read a classic you've started and stopped since college, or urge surf.

2. While engaging in mastery muscle building, be mindful. Notice what you are doing and stay in the moment with it. Mile three is simply (and perfectly) mile three, not a countdown to mile twenty-six. You don't need to analyze your performance. Let go of judgments. This is a time to increase your range of what you believe is possible. Cheer yourself on.

3. Gradually increase the difficulty of the goal you pursue over time.

♥

Practicing Nonjudgmental Mastery

Nonjudgmental mastery may sound like a paradox—how are you aware of advancing and becoming increasingly competent if you don't judge? Similarly, not judging urges may seem counterintuitive. Well, facts are the antithesis of judgment. "I ran five miles this week and last week I ran four miles" is not a judgment, it's a matter of fact. Observing, "I sat with my emotions," is also a statement of fact. Describing facts is not judging, and it can be free of the psychological side effects of judging. When you label yourself as having had a "bad" run, how likely are you to either return to the track or notice your mood improve? Similarly, labeling urges as "bad" will increase your struggle. However, considering, "Is engaging in this urge *effective*?" may facilitate positive action.

Mastery is not achieved to get rid of a negative emotional state or prevent a new one. Trying to force yourself to feel other than you do will maintain feeling X and add feeling Y. You feel sad and you work on a *New York Times* crossword puzzle, wishing you could feel better, and then you feel sad and frustrated. The alternative is noticing you feel sad, accepting the feeling, and fully engaging in the crossword puzzle for the sake of mastery, not to minimize your sadness.

Summary

As this chapter comes to an end, let's review a couple of main principles. Urges and emotions are part of living, and both of them ebb and flow. We can step back and notice how they change in magnitude over time. We get ensnared when we seek instant fixes, such as eating to get rid of difficult emotions. The ability to observe our emotions and urges builds our sense of mastery. And the more we change our behaviors, the more habitual this will become, widening our options. *Surfing urges creates mastery. Mastery requires surfing urges.* Don't get me wrong—expanding your comfort zone is not easy. But the results may be exhilarating. The world is your marathon, and day by day you can make the decision to master the miles and surf the pain.

Chapter 6

MINDING YOUR MIND

It is far more difficult to murder a phantom than a reality.

—VIRGINIA WOOLF

Many people who struggle with difficult feelings and with eating problems engage in thinking that is judgmental, categorical, and repetitive. Are you aware of holding on to thoughts that no longer serve you? We've reviewed how thoughts or interpretations can create feelings and influence behavior. In this chapter, we'll explore the possibility of freeing yourself from difficult emotions by changing your relationship with thinking.

Have you ever observed a gentle elderly man as he watches children, perhaps his own grandchildren, playing in the park? How might he watch the children play? If a child began struggling with difficult emotions, would the older man approach and scold, "You're upset about a stupid sandcastle. Do you know what alimony means?" The prospect of that occurring is so absurd it's humorous. An elder watching children play would likely notice with so much kindness, wisdom, and perspective.

In the most respectful way, I invite you to consider the prospect of noticing your thoughts as you'd imagine an elder would watch a child playing in the sand—with curiosity, distance, and wisdom. Of course many of your thoughts serve you. At other times you may find yourself caught in unproductive, painful mental traps that feel imprisoning, when the ability to release yourself lies within you.

The Problem with Thinking

Only humans can bring negative events into any setting at any moment. You may be on a wonderful vacation, when suddenly you think of a lost loved one, and experience pain. When you think about food, even when it is not in your presence, you may notice your mouth water and you may find yourself struggling in deciding whether or not to eat. In the absence of physical hunger, you may notice fantasizing about food, feel stuck on this fantasy in your mind, and go out of your way to eat.

Language and cognition are based on the capacity to relate events to each other. While speaking and analyzing are often instrumental to many aspects of our lives, they may also prove detrimental. You may find yourself making arbitrary connections, and because the process of connecting is so essential to how our brains work, you may lose contact with the fact that your connections aren't necessarily true. Yet your mind may hold on to such ideas and relationships as factual. You may decide nothing will work because your efforts so far haven't succeeded. Simply having the thought "Nothing will work" may engender feelings of helplessness and get in the way of your pursuing behaviors to move ahead.

What is the thought "Nothing will work?" In a sense it's just a combination of words and letters. Yet relating to that thought as though it were valid and meaningful can lead to painful feelings and urges to give up, which can in turn drive behaviors that shape your life. How often have you noticed yourself caught up in thoughts and later realized the thoughts were simply untrue? Years ago, as a student, I frequently experienced worry thoughts around failure. During my orientation as a doctoral student, our dean told us that several people would not pass the first semester. I immediately began to think, "Oh no, what will I do next semester?" And this sort of thinking often came up without any evidence to substantiate my fears. A thought is a thought, an idea that evidence may or may not support. In contrast, a fact is substantiated with evidence. To differentiate thoughts from facts, it may be useful to ask yourself, "Would this hold up in a court of law?" Would a jury unanimously conclude, "Nothing will work?"

There is a big difference between noticing thoughts and believing thoughts. The first is mindful and opens up many possibilities for choosing behaviors; the second is not mindful and can lock us into habitual behaviors.

Exercise: Thinking vs. Believing

1. For a moment, consider a thought that comes up often, and regard the thought as simply a thought rather than a fact.

2. If you treated this thought as a fact, how might you act?

3. If you actually believed that this thought was simply a thought, how might you act?

4. What would happen if you were to let go of some of your other thoughts or begin to change your relationship with your thinking?

It's important to bring awareness to your thoughts around your ability to sit with feelings and to your thoughts around food and your shape. Do you believe any of the following common thoughts?

- ☐ If I am thin, I'll be happy.

- ☐ I need to wait until I have better control over my feelings and eating before I can be social.

- ☐ I can't help but sabotage myself.

- ☐ If I say no to eating something someone made for me, I will hurt his feelings.

- ☐ If I don't finish what's on my plate, I am wasteful.

- ☐ I have no control over my life if I can't control my eating.

- ☐ I need to wait until my body is perfect before I can _____ .

- ☐ I can't do anything until I'm motivated.

☐   I don't deserve to buy nice clothes that make me feel comfortable until I am a size _____ .

☐   Feeling fat means I'm worthless and lazy.

☐   I can't control my impulses.

☐   If I messed up, there is no point in trying to turn it around. I might as well enjoy giving up until tomorrow.

♥

You may notice all the thoughts in the checklist in the preceding exercise are similar in that they are categorical—that is, they exemplify all-or-nothing thinking, lacking flexibility or awareness of alternative vantage points.

If one of the thoughts listed above is a thought that you notice often, can you notice how the thought may not be a fact? If you experience a thought that is extreme, what may be a more flexible way of thinking about the same subject? For example, you may replace the thought "I can't control my impulses" with a more flexible statement, such as "Sometimes it feels hard to sit with impulses." You can change your relationship with thinking by noticing extreme thoughts and considering more flexible interpretations or simply by changing your relationship with thinking by taking thoughts less literally.

Common Thinking Traps

Many people struggle with particular types of judgmental thoughts. It may be helpful to notice when you begin to engage in some common thinking patterns, described below.

Comparisons

Comparing aspects of yourself, including your body, to someone else can often lead to negative feelings. When you compare, there is often a judgmental quality in your attention. Have comparisons ever been helpful to you? Interestingly enough, comparisons may be useful if you compare your current situation to a time you struggled more, or if you compare yourself to others who are less fortunate. That sort of comparison can cultivate gratitude.

However, often comparisons entail judging yourself against someone especially thin or attractive, perhaps a celebrity or the most beautiful person you know. You may fail to notice the average person. Whom do you compare yourself to? Does your reference point set you up for disappointment? If you find yourself stuck in the habit of comparing yourself to others, you may notice when you are comparing, then practice mindfully returning to the moment by letting go of judgments. If this seems too difficult, you may practice moving away from extreme comparisons toward ones that are more sensible. Many of my affluent clients actually complain a lot about not having enough money. They compare themselves to their wealthiest friends, who own four homes, rather than noticing where they stand across the full spectrum of people, including people who are struggling financially or homeless. Similarly, you may notice that you compare yourself to a unique group rather than to the average person or every fourth person you see. When you compare yourself only to people who appear perfect, how do you feel? If you compared yourself to every fourth person you noticed, how might you feel?

Exercise: Noticing Comparisons

1. Is there a particular situation (like going to the beach, eating a meal with others, or sitting with difficult feelings) where you find yourself consumed with unhelpful comparisons ("No one has it as bad as I do")?

2. Practice bringing awareness to the fact that you are comparing. Simply notice the fact, label it "comparing," and practice letting go of judgments, perhaps by focusing on your breath.

♥

Perfectionism

Many people hold on to thoughts about needing to be perfect—and also tightly hold on to certain narrow definitions of perfection. You may hold yourself to very high standards in terms of appearance or goals to achieve. Do you judge yourself according to how much you achieve and find yourself thinking a lot about your performance? Certain behaviors closely relate to thoughts about needing to be perfect. For example, you may repeatedly check how you are doing or spend a lot of time trying to analyze how you are doing compared to someone else. Some people who aim to do their very best find themselves avoiding tasks out of fear that they won't do well enough. If you are a perfectionist, you may see things in *all-or-nothing terms*—you are either perfect or a failure. There is also a tendency in perfectionism to *catastrophize*—in other words, you may see a single event as more than just a single event. For example, if you eat for emotional reasons, you may consider yourself a "total mess."

Exercise: Sticky Notes

For this exercise you'll need both small sticky notes and a sheet of paper (inspired by the chessboard metaphor in Hayes, Strosahl, and Wilson 1999).

1. Bring to mind thoughts you often have about yourself, both good and bad.

2. On different small sticky notes, write down the thoughts you have. For example, one note may say "good friend"; another may say "emotional eater"; another may say "crazy mom."

3. After you write the thoughts that you notice often—we'll call them sticky thoughts—on sticky notes, place all these sticky notes on a sheet of paper.

4. Now spend a minute trying to figure out which sticky note on the paper really defines you. Using the example above, are you "emotional eater" or "good friend"? Who are you really?

Do your positive thoughts reign? Or do you identify more with your negative thoughts about yourself?

5. What if you stepped back for a moment and considered that these sticky notes aren't really you? What else might you be? What if you are the piece of paper, rather than a single sticky note? A helpful way to change your relationship with thoughts about who you are and how you need to be is to see yourself as more than just thoughts, feelings, or accomplishments. Thoughts pass through us, but we are not thoughts, no matter how sticky the thoughts may feel.

♥

Rumination

Rumination describes a way people try to cope with distress and entails repeatedly thinking over a negative thought or memory. "Rumination" stems from the Latin *ruminari,* meaning to chew over, like a cow on its cud. Both feelings and thoughts typically arise, peak, and fade—unless you cling to them or ruminate on them.

Rumination is a recipe for depression and disordered eating. The mental act of chewing over results in the physical act of chewing! Rumination is actually a form of avoidance—when you ruminate, you are less focused on directly experiencing and expressing the current emotion and are more caught up in an abstract story. You can think of rumination as a way to try to analyze and control thinking. Does it help? It may often be as pointless as worry, to which it is similar. Worry anticipates problems in the future, whereas the content of rumination is the past. For example, rather than attending to how you feel in this moment about an argument with your partner, when ruminating you are instead overcome with such thoughts as: "No one treats me well. Since we've been together I've never been a priority. This reminds me of how I felt as a child…" Rumination builds a mountain of evidence for hopelessness; consider it the opposite of active problem solving (Nolen-Hoeksema, Wisco, and Lyubomirsky 2008). What if after an argument with your partner you walked the dog, bringing your full attention to sensations in your body and observing details outside yourself on your walk, and when your emotions came down, you considered practical ways to problem solve with your partner? Or, you may recognize in the aftermath of an argument that emotions are colored by conflict—and bring that awareness into the present. Susan Nolen-Hoeksema, a psychologist at Yale University, has pioneered research on rumination and discovered that it impairs problem solving, predicts depression, and erodes social support (Nolen-Hoeksema, Wisco, and Lyubomirsky 2008). Who wants to hear the same story over and over? Even you yourself should not be subjected to that.

Leila's Story

Leila is an actress who struggles with feeling depressed. She thinks a lot about how she has failed to meet her aspirations and accumulate accolades. At one time, Leila enjoyed watching TV to relax and as a means of generating ideas to write and produce. Eventually, however, seeing other actors on TV accentuated Leila's pain over not working herself. At a certain point, Leila found watching sitcoms painful and avoided TV. This ultimately led to her spending more and more time trying to figure out why she was depressed. And this led to Leila's seeking the instant gratification of unhealthy foods. But the foods did not stop her endless thoughts. Leila continued to ruminate on disappointments and pains, starting from childhood and ending in this moment (her weight gain offered another source of pain). She also figured that it would be worthwhile to share her pain. So she would repeatedly tell her husband, Ben, how unsuccessful and unworthy she felt. He tried as best he could to be patient and helpful, but Leila's reassurance seeking exhausted him. "How can you love me given no one wants to work with me?" she'd ask. "Well, you're a great partner and fantastic person." "Maybe you just don't know me that well," she'd retort. Ben, understandably, grew frustrated with her persistent negativity. Then Leila began worrying about Ben's being annoyed with her. Now she was "failing" at work, at eating sensibly, and at love itself. This sort of thinking became the mental equivalent of riding the teacups at an amusement park: a fast, nauseating ride going nowhere.

Do you ruminate on food and your shape? You may start by ruminating on feelings, then eat in response to your own ruminations, and then ruminate about eating. Rumination is an activity that easily finds a topic. "I can't find a job. It's not fair that I have a slow metabolism and can't eat enough to fill me up. I'm hungry but yesterday I ate a bit too much. I wonder if I should skip a meal or if that will slow my metabolism. Things usually don't work out when I try; why should I bother?" Notice how circular thinking is unclear? To be frank, rumination is ruination!

It is no coincidence that rumination is strongly related to suppression, avoidance, distress, and binge eating. Studies have found rumination to predict bulimic behaviors and binge eating in adolescent girls (Nolen-Hoeksema et al. 2007). Eating disorders are characterized by rumination, the belief that rumination is helpful, and avoidance of experiences (Rawal, Park, and Williams 2010). Ruminating on shape, weight, or food can serve to distract you or help you avoid difficult emotions or relationships. It may be easier to think a lot about food instead of a painful past. The problem is that you then experience pain around food.

Lucy tried to explain a recent episode of emotional eating: "A few days ago I ordered a burrito, and there was a minimum delivery order of two. I thought it was stupid to order two since I'm trying to count calories and it seems like a lot and I don't love them. Then I was bored and had the second burrito I meant to have tomorrow, though I wasn't hungry. I can't stop eating when I'm bored if food is around.... My mom was like that too. I figured it makes no sense to keep track of food since it's usually like this. I have no control and have too much weight to lose and I'm not willing to wait. Why bother?" Notice how thinking and analyzing entrap her? Problem solving or fully contacting the present moment rather than getting stuck in stories is often more helpful. As Voltaire said, "Let us work without theorizing, 'tis the only way to make life endurable."

Do you notice when you are ruminating? Often, when you find yourself in a place where emotions govern thinking, you may find yourself ruminating. Noticing and labeling "emotion mind" or "ruminating" may be helpful in bringing you back to this moment. One way to let go of rumination is to look *at* thoughts, rather than *from* thoughts. Practice this with the following mindfulness exercise.

Exercise: Mindfulness Practice— Leaves on a Stream

1. Assume a mindful seat in a chair, with your spine upright and your feet either flat on the ground if you are sitting in a chair or folded comfortably if you are sitting on the floor or a cushion.

2. Close your eyes and bring your full attention to your breathing, just attending to one inhale and exhale at a time.

3. Next, bring your attention to where your body touches your seat.

4. Notice that there is no effort required in practicing being where you are.

5. Now, bring to mind a beautiful park.

6. In this mental image, notice a tree in the distance.

7. Imagine walking toward the tree, becoming more present in the moment with each step.

8. Imagine that there is a river beside the tree.

9. Can you picture yourself sitting beside the river on a warm autumn day watching leaves float downstream?

10. Now, bring your awareness to your thoughts.

11. Each time a thought or an image arrives in your mind, gently place the thought or image on a leaf.

12. Try to sit and be with the tree, and when a thought arrives that takes you away from being fully present ("Am I doing this right?"), place that thought on a leaf.

13. If thoughts aren't arriving, notice that thought, "I'm not having thoughts," and place it on a leaf.

14. Without any struggle, thoughts arrive and depart.

15. Notice what it's like to watch thoughts from this more detached place, where you look *at* thoughts rather than *from* thoughts.

16. After a few minutes of watching leaves float down the river, bring your awareness back to your breath. Breathe deeply.

17. Begin to let go of this image, bringing your awareness back to your sensations and surroundings in the present moment as you open your eyes.

18. Can you carry this sense of awareness of thoughts as you move through your day?

(Adapted from Hayes and Smith 2005)

♥

The Problem with Trying to Control Thinking

The alternative to either holding onto thoughts (ruminating) or flexibly letting go of thoughts (accepting) is trying to rigidly stop thoughts (suppressing). What are your beliefs about thoughts? Do you believe that you must keep negative thoughts under surveillance? Deliberate attempts to stop thinking are not effective. Notice what happens when you try not to think about RED VELVET CUPCAKES. Trying not to think of RED VELVET CUPCAKES is in fact a thought about red velvet cupcakes. Suppression includes constant monitoring, or engaging with the thought, preparing us to notice it more. Studies (e.g., Wegner 1994) have found that suppression actually increases the frequency of the thought one is trying to suppress and also increases the level of distress around the thought.

Ironically, thought suppression both causes and maintains depression, general anxiety, social anxiety, and obsessive-compulsive disorder (Purdon 1999). How do you relate to your thoughts?

Do you ever try to suppress thoughts around food? Often, people who diet try to suppress thoughts around food. This is counterproductive in the end. In fact, suppressing food thoughts predicts food cravings and binge eating (Barnes and Tantleff-Dunn 2010). When energy is expended trying to control thinking, less is available to regulate behaviors. Food may be a way to escape from thoughts, especially if you are suppressing them and then experiencing a whole family of the thought returning with more strength and momentum. Alternatively, you may have some flexibility around a thought. *If you let go of trying to control thinking, paradoxically, you retain control.*

Accepting Thoughts

Interestingly, a helpful way to manage thinking is by accepting thoughts. If you struggle with worry, it can be helpful to be willing to have worry (Borkovec and Sharpless 2004). What would happen if you changed your relationship with worry by noticing thoughts as events rather than alarms? In one scientifically supported treatment, individuals who struggle with painful intrusive thoughts are encouraged to sing their thoughts (Foa and Wilson 2001)!

Imagine singing "There's something really wrong with me" to the tune of your favorite Beatles song. How would you feel? Now consider how you would feel if your life's purpose was to avoid facing that thought and you also stopped moving toward what you care about because of the thought. There are ways to change your relationship with both thoughts and the stories you may tell yourself so that they do not govern your mind and body.

Reigning with RAIN

Many Buddhist teachers describe RAIN, a helpful mindfulness tool that may promote sitting with thoughts as well as feelings or urges.

R—*Recognize* what is happening. Notice thoughts, feelings, and sensations in this moment. What is happening now? This may be a gentle reminder to return to this moment with curiosity and openness.

A—*Accept or allow* life as it is. This includes allowing thoughts, emotions, and feelings. When you fully accept and stay in the present moment, it's not possible to ruminate, suppress, or judgmentally compare. Acceptance may be challenging when you notice you face something aversive. You may ask yourself, "May I sit with this in this moment?"

I—*Investigate* inner experience. Investigation includes a sense of nonjudgmental interest: "What thoughts am I buying into? What am I feeling?" This requires slowing down rather than automatically reacting. Rather than getting caught in the thought or feeling, you're noticing it and aware of subtle changes in your body: "I'm having the thought that I can't sit with this urge to eat. I notice my mouth watering." When investigating, there's a quality of kindness in your awareness, quite distinct from an "Oh no, not again" attitude.

N—*Not identifying* with the thought or feeling. You are not your thoughts and feelings. Your sense of self is broader than the stories of your mind. As in the exercise earlier in the chapter, you are the paper—larger than and distinct and separate from small and impermanent sticky notes. When you perceive yourself as more than transient thoughts, sensations, or desires, you have more power to live with choice.

Jared's Story

When Jared feels lonely and stressed after a long day of classes, he often stops at a drug store and stocks up on chips and cookies. When he doesn't have plans or thinks he has little choice, if he has intense thoughts around food, he feels as though he has to eat. With practice, Jared begins to *recognize* thoughts, feelings, and sensations as he leaves his evening class and walks home. He notices such thoughts as "I need to eat"; feelings including loneliness and anxiety; and also tension in his body. He *allows* these thoughts and feelings to pass without trying to indulge or get rid of them. Upon slowing down, he *investigates*, discerning that this is part of what his mind and body do after class when he feels lonely and food thoughts arrive in his mind. Jared practices *not identifying* with the thoughts. He doesn't feel attached to them or controlled by them; he simply notices thoughts and feelings and practices expanding his awareness to notice where he is in the moment, the temperature in the air, people walking on the street, and his breath. By expanding his awareness, he notices the full landscape of his experience instead of developing tunnel vision around a particular sticky thought.

Exercise: Practice RAIN

Describe a situation where you feel caught up in your thoughts and apply RAIN.

R—What do you *recognize* in this moment?

A—How are you practicing *acceptance*?

I—How might you nonjudgmentally *investigate* your experience?

N—How might you expand your *natural awareness* to not define yourself by thoughts or feelings?

♥

Summary

Marcus Aurelius said, "The soul becomes dyed with the color of its thoughts." The main problem with thinking is when we fail to see the process of thinking as just that—thinking. Similarly, it's helpful to also notice that feelings are feelings and that remembering is just remembering. This is the benefit in practicing mindfulness. You can remember that thoughts are thoughts, not actions or facts. A lot of suffering arises when you narrow your awareness and get lost in the painful stories in your mind. Watch the children play in your mind's playground with kindness and perspective. You can't choose what arrives in your mind, though you can choose how you pay attention to internal events and also how you respond. If you host a party and some unwanted guests arrive, would you rather spend the night consumed with anger about the party crashers, watching them roam from room to room, or enjoying the rest of the party and conversing with people you care about? You can better enjoy life's party when you're not weighed down trying to control unwanted visitors who may actually leave, if you neither taunt them nor seat them, after a few minutes.

Chapter 7

COPING WITH DIFFICULT EMOTIONS WITHOUT A SECOND HELPING

Things falling apart is a kind of testing and also a kind of healing. We think that the point is to pass the test or to overcome the problem, but the truth is that things don't really get solved. They come together and they fall apart. Then they come together and fall apart again. It's just like that. The healing comes from letting there be room for all of this to happen: room for grief, for relief, for misery, for joy.

—PEMA CHÖDRÖN

You are sitting in a brightly decorated ice cream parlor. Your friend owns the dessert bar; it's his store's first anniversary party, and you are feeling remarkably anxious as you greet a crowd of sweet-toothed strangers. Waiters offer you a milkshake to drink and you're encouraged to line up for ice cream. Vanilla lavender, green tea, Belgian chocolate—the options seem endless. You may either drink the milkshake or refuse it, but it looks like you'll need to participate in the ice cream tasting. If you drink the milkshake, will you eat more or less ice cream? Will you choose a lighter option or go for multiple scoops? Put yourself in the situation: what would you do?

In a 1975 study, researchers C. Peter Herman and Debbie Mack told women they were analyzing "taste" and offered them the choice of consuming zero, one, or two milkshakes. Later, the women were allowed to eat as much ice cream as they wanted. Unbeknownst to the participants, this study actually looked at eating habits rather than taste. For the most part, women who had the milkshakes ate less ice cream during the "taste test." This makes sense, given that they may have felt satiated by having had some ice cream in the milkshake. However, the women who were on diets ate *more* ice cream after they consumed a milkshake. Researchers call this the "disinhibition effect." People who try to limit what they eat may feel quite guilty, paradoxically prompting them to actually eat more. In other words, you engage in a behavior, feel bad, and end up engaging in more behaviors that may make you feel worse. Also, if you eat for emotional reasons, you may continue to eat to avoid experiencing emotions. *Eating* even serves as a way to cope with negative emotions that arise from *eating* (Herman and Polivy 2004).

Now add intense emotions to the scenario. When you feel intensely, break a diet rule, and experience more intense emotions around eating, this may culminate in more emotions and more eating. In this chapter, you will learn ways to cope with intense emotions without reacting impulsively or reaching for more ice cream after you drink a milkshake.

Impulse: Do Bad Moods Make for Bad Decisions?

On a rational level, adding up impulsive behaviors or making mood-driven decisions makes little sense. However, emotionally, you may notice the tendency or drive to engage in impulsive behaviors when you experience negative emotions.

Numerous patients over the years have told me they "self-sabotage" and believe that this tendency to engage in self-defeating behaviors derives from an unconscious desire to fail. Is this really the case? When we consider what happens when we respond to difficult emotions with risky behavior, this impulsivity makes sense, even in the absence of complicated analytical theories.

Often, when we are upset, we may deliberately choose to pursue a risky behavior because we have placed a premium on ridding ourselves of a difficult emotion. For example, in the face of loneliness, people may resort to calling a complicated ex in hopes of zapping the loneliness of the moment. In negative mood states, the focus is often myopic, with your attention on the goal "Get me out of here." You might fail to consider how you may feel the day after you spend time with the ex—or how you may feel if your advance is unreciprocated. When you face a difficult emotion, such as loneliness, you may find yourself so determined to rid yourself of that feeling that you don't really think through the costs of such briefly distracting behavior.

We don't wish to "self-sabotage"; we wish to "self-soothe" and "feel better," yet the ways we do so—nonacceptance of emotions and impulsive behavior—actually make us feel worse over time. When people are in a bad mood, they are more likely to engage in risky behavior. In a study, when participants felt embarrassed, they were more likely to participate in a high-risk, high-payoff lottery than a low-risk, low-payoff option (Leith and Baumeister 1996). In choosing a high-risk choice, you face a reduced chance that you may actually win money and escape a negative mood. You also face the increased chance that you won't win anything and will end up feeling worse than when you began.

Negative emotions are not the problem—they are emblematic of being alive. It's what you do when they arrive that can create unnecessary pain. Nonacceptance is the culprit again! As explored in chapter 2, nonacceptance increases emotional suffering. Now, we're expanding our understanding, and clarifying emotions may not be as problematic as nonacceptance of the emotion and the behaviors symptomatic of nonacceptance. These behaviors—calling the ex or grabbing the spoon—are what actually make things worse.

Poor Mood, Poor Thinking

Often, negative mood states affect thinking. It is helpful to keep this in mind given what we know about the tendency for moods to affect impulsive behaviors. Psychologists who measure intelligence take into account the fact that when someone is notably depressed or anxious, IQ scores fall. This again reflects the concept that "emotion mind" is distinct from "reasonable mind."

In one study (Baumeister, Nuss, and Twenge 2002), researchers convincingly (and falsely) told participants that they would end up alone later in life, then had them take intelligence tests, to look at the effect the thought of being alone (a disturbing notion for most people) has on intelligence. Participants scored significantly below their capacity on measures of intelligence after hearing the depressing prediction made. The authors theorize that the subjects' spending mental energy suppressing feelings or ruminating on being alone made less mental energy available for other tasks.

When we're struggling with notably difficult feelings, such as those engendered by the thought "I will end up alone," it can be important to remember to consciously slow down. Otherwise, your energy may be depleted managing your emotions, and your thinking may not be helpful in problem solving. A client of mine described a police officer pulling her over for erratic driving, assuming that she was drunk. Her friend had just tragically and unexpectedly died. There was no alcohol in her system, but sorrow similarly steered her thinking away from the road.

The combination of painful emotions, difficulty sitting with emotions, and urgency to escape feelings while thinking unintelligently may thus lead to impulsive actions—and yet more painful feelings.

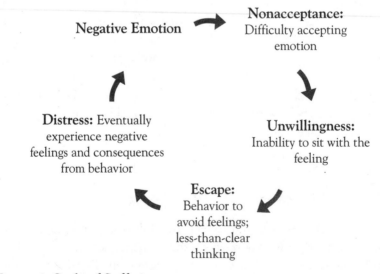

Figure 4: Cycle of Suffering

Grace: Pain with Poise

In any emotional situation we face, there is an opportunity to cope with emotions with grace. I love the word "grace." It implies willingness and wisdom; quite different than "impulse." We all face the choice of accepting reality or emotions with grace or trying to escape our feelings, perhaps through indulging our impulses.

One of the main premises of this book, and the essence of much of the research that supports the ideas we've reviewed, is that people who struggle with difficult feelings tend to use food to cope. In this chapter, you'll learn to slow down around difficult emotions with graceful action. When you accept pain, you suffer less. When you avoid pain, you exacerbate it and experience secondary emotions and may engage in problematic behaviors that create more pain.

What Is Distress Tolerance?

Distress tolerance refers to the ability to accept and cope well with difficult emotions given that we can't avoid pain and that impulsive behaviors will increase pain (Linehan 1993b). Distress tolerance refers to both your *perception* of your ability to sit with physical or emotional pain and also the *behavior* of tolerating difficult feelings (Leyro, Zvolensky, and Bernstein 2010).

When I say "your perception," I don't mean you need a mass of confidence. As reviewed in the last chapter, the five letters in the phrase "I can't" won't thwart you unless you let a couple of words govern your mind and body. You may instead hold on lightly to stories about what you are and are not capable of and commit to thoughtfully acting consistently with your values. Of course, this feels challenging, and it requires skill and practice.

Exercise: Examples of Difficulties with Distress Tolerance

If you are wondering whether you struggle with sitting with intense emotions, use this checklist to help you consider your thoughts and feelings surrounding them. Do you agree with any of the following statements?

- ☐ My feelings overwhelm me.

- ☐ I can't accept painful emotions.

- ☐ I can't stop thinking about my problems or painful feelings.

- ☐ When I feel strongly, I lose control and act very impulsively.

- ☐ I notice I go from feeling bad to feeling terrible because of the way I cope.

- ☐ I am embarrassed by my intense feelings.

- ☐ No one else feels the way I do.

- ☐ Distracting myself from an emotion is better than feeling it.

♥

In the preceding checklist, notice the relationship between difficulties with distress tolerance and not accepting emotions or coping with them flexibly. A lot of what we have explored in previous chapters acts as foundational steps in the complex dance of distress tolerance. In the dance of distress tolerance, steps include acceptance, mindfulness, noticing emotions, and surfing urges. Distress tolerance is impossible without cultivating mindfulness in order to notice emotions, notice urges, and accept pain. You can't prevent a crisis from building without awareness and acceptance. Also, since distress tolerance has to do with your perception of your ability to cope, it's helpful to bring a lot of awareness to your thoughts. Finally, awareness of your values (which we'll discuss in chapter 9) and commitment to the values you choose sets your range of responses.

After all, behaviors you might engage in while in emotional distress are problematic when they move you away from what matters to you.

How is distress tolerance any different from emotion regulation? In both cases, again, each step requires mindfulness. Emotion regulation applies to the ordinary experience of emotion; distress tolerance pertains to emotions that feel extraordinarily overwhelming. Distress tolerance requires all the tools you've learned in previous chapters. Emotion regulation requires coordination; the choreography of distress tolerance is trickier and the music less melodious. A greater degree of pain requires more precise coordination, and later in this chapter you'll learn that the coordination required is actually a graceful slowing down.

When you notice emotions that are high (say, above 7 on a scale of 1 to 10, where 10 is extremely intense), this is when you know distress tolerance is needed. It can be challenging to notice emotions and consider how strongly you feel, given that emotions climb quickly.

Exercise: Noticing Intense Emotions

Reflect back on this week or your recent history and notice for a moment situations where your emotions felt overwhelming. In addition to noticing the emotion, you can also bring to mind urges associated with the experience. Next, you can note how you feel now about either engaging in the action associated with the strong emotion or choosing to surf the action urge.

For example, looking back on the week, you notice feeling anxiety at the level of 8 when thinking about having to give a presentation at work. Your urge included overeating and procrastinating, and you both binged and procrastinated on the task by surfing the Internet for hours. Now, you feel aware that those behaviors did not serve you, as you had to stay up all night and felt sick to your stomach, making it more difficult to prepare and present.

In noticing, you are not judging—you are simply noticing with the wisdom of perspective which actions intense emotions move you away from or toward.

1. Describe the situation.

2. What was the emotion, and how intense was it, on a scale of 1 to 10, with 10 being extremely intense?

3. What action urges did you experience? What actual actions did you take?

4. What are your nonjudgmental thoughts and feelings on the actions you took?

Every person experiences emotions uniquely. One person's heartache may feel like heartbreak to another. Here we are talking about how you feel, not what you perceive as "normal." Some people describe feeling overwhelmed and impulsive when facing extraordinarily positive emotions, such as joy or love, as well as negative ones. When emotions feel overwhelming to you, you might need to focus on tolerating distress by practicing acceptance and self-soothing as a first step in preparation for regulating emotions. Opposite action, noticing interpretations, confronting a friend about a disagreement, or practicing a formal mindful meditation of the breath often feels impossible in the midst of an emotional avalanche, when the mind races aimlessly. Distress tolerance allows you to recharge before reacting.

♥

Distress Tolerance and Emotional Eating

If you believe that you cannot cope with difficult emotions and urgently want to get rid of pain, then understandably you may overly rely on eating. You want an instant emotional fix; food is an instant source of both distraction and pleasure—it's everywhere. This is a recipe for eating to cope. Relying on eating to cope with emotions may interfere with cultivating alternative ways to cope, and lack of coping tools maintains problematic eating. Notice (as reviewed in earlier chapters) that how what we use to solve a problem often maintains the struggle. Emotional eating is like trying to lift the stain of a pen with a thick, permanent marker.

Practicing Distress Tolerance

So far, we've explored how difficulty sitting with extraordinary emotions can lead to behaviors that actually make things worse over time. If crises are maintained by nonacceptance of emotions and resulting behaviors, distress tolerance entails learning to slow down to accept what is and at the same time learning to improve the moment in the absence of crisis-generating behaviors (Linehan 1993b). You can't control thoughts and feelings, though you can choose how you greet them.

You may apply distress tolerance in all of the following scenarios:

1. Sitting with overwhelming emotions

2. Coping with emotions that arise in response to behaviors you've engaged in

3. Accepting the pain that stems from letting go of routine behaviors

For example, when you feel jealous of a friend who seems to enjoy all life's riches, you may practice distress tolerance to sit with those feelings. If you did not practice distress tolerance at that point, and you impulsively overate, you may practice distress tolerance to cope with both your feelings of envy and your guilt around eating. At any point, you may practice distress tolerance in sitting with the discomfort of not engaging in an urge. Many people understandably struggle with overwhelming feelings, thoughts, and sensations when changing routine behaviors. If you give up smoking, you may similarly practice distress tolerance in sitting with difficult feelings when they arise. You can also practice distress tolerance if you do smoke a cigarette, to help you stop before you smoke a pack. And of course distress tolerance is needed to cope with the discomfort of nicotine withdrawal.

Gia's Story

Gia is a mother of hyperactive twins with learning disabilities. She often finds herself flooded with irritation. Often, she finds binge eating the only activity she can engage in to cope with her frustration when the boys refuse to do their homework and whine. She finds herself angry about feeling impatient and turning to eating. Then she feels sad about overeating and feeling fat and "out of control." When she feels overwhelmingly sad, she's unable to help the boys with their homework and retreats to her room, saying she is unwell. Then she feels anxious about being a "neglectful" mom and goes to bed, asking her babysitter to take charge, then snacks more the next morning. "Why bother trying?" she ruminates. "I'm angry, lazy, and out of control."

In learning distress tolerance in therapy, Gia learned that coping with overwhelming emotions was not an all-or-nothing feat. She committed to practicing accepting the irritation that inevitably arose. When she didn't catch herself judging her emotions and exacerbating them, but ate for emotional reasons, she practiced soothing herself in ways that were helpful in getting her back to the boys before she retreated to her room. She found that rubbing her forehead with a cold towel she sprayed with a eucalyptus scent was a refreshing and quick break that didn't get in the way of her values as a mom. Gia described feeling empowered, knowing that her emotions would not dictate her action, which challenged her long-held belief that "experiencing emotions equals being snatched by them." She became more flexible, noticing contentedly times she did not retreat after eating but stayed present with the boys.

At any point, practicing distress tolerance might save you from emotional quicksand. And the way you practice distress tolerance is similar to the way you might get out of quicksand—slow, deliberate movements.

Negative Emotion → **Acceptance:** Practice awareness and acceptance of the emotion

Choose Grace: Actively practice acceptance and self-soothing

Willingness: Practice opening yourself up to sitting with discomfort

Notice: Slow down to observe urges to eat or to avoid, and also to bring awareness to what you value

Figure 5: Cycle of Self-Compassionate Slowing Down

Tools to Tolerate Distress

Coping with a crisis can feel like standing on your head. Interestingly, in order to stand on your head, you actually bear no weight on your head. Grounding your forearms and engaging your abdomen, back, mind, and breath provide full support to carry your weight upside down. Similarly, in a crisis situation, connecting with your breath, core values, and mindfulness skills is more effective than deliberately applying pressure with your head. You cannot think your way out of a crisis. You can possess the wisdom to know it's time to engage all your tools until you are in a mind state conducive to problem solving.

Now, let's review specific skills to cope with a crisis with grace, just as you'd engage all your muscles intelligently to stand on your head. Many of these skills are based on Marsha Linehan's (1993b) teachings on distress tolerance, and thousands of people have found these strategies remarkably helpful. Distress tolerance skills entail a complete synthesis of accepting and soothing.

Accountability

Many thoughtful people over the years have asked me why we focus on soothing if soothing may serve as a distraction. Is soothing the same as avoiding? While soothing may feel distracting, functionally, it's different from avoiding. You're not running away or escaping your feelings. Rather, you notice pain, accept pain, and mindfully choose to take care of yourself in the service of moving forward. You may think of using soothing skills as making a pit stop: it's a needed pause but not a final destination. Also keep in mind that employing these tools throughout your travels may facilitate your traveling well. This is analogous to stopping for gas on a journey or taking a moment to catch your breath. If you're participating in athletic training, you should train in a way that allows you to move forward each day; train too hard and you risk injury.

This may also be a matter of degree. For example, if you feel really sad and choose to take a break from your obligations, listening to a couple of peppy songs may be soothing. Listening to music for forty minutes, however, may entail avoidance. If you feel lonely and want to soothe yourself and feel connected, you might check your e-mail for twenty minutes. Checking your e-mail and surfing the Internet for hours and "forgetting" about the Pilates class you signed up for is clearly avoidance. Taking a nap after a red-eye serves as self-care, and this differs from sleeping for hours during the day to escape sad feelings. Similarly, eating may invigorate or fatigue, depending on the portion. Soothing as a distress tolerance tool requires mindfully noticing and honestly holding yourself accountable: is this moving you toward or away from what matters?

Accountability is relevant to distress tolerance skills, given that engaging in a "soothing" behavior can get you further stuck in distress. Procrastinating, overeating, compulsive spending, and pursuing promiscuous sex exemplify the ways "escapes" escort us toward crises.

Acceptance Revisited

As discussed throughout this book, acceptance and willingness are essential in coping with both ordinary emotions and extraordinarily difficult ones, as well as with urges of all magnitudes. Now, we'll explore additional opportunities to practice acceptance; opportunities that often feel challenging in a crisis.

Accepting Food Cravings

Evan Forman and his colleagues (2007) at Drexel University studied ninety-eight college students who described enjoying chocolate. The students were given a clear box of Hershey's Kisses and told not to eat them and to return them to the experimenters after forty-eight hours. (One of the reasons this example is in this section is because seeing a chocolate in a store may spur urges; imagine the cravings you'd encounter in carrying chocolate on you for two days!)

The experimenters cleverly marked each chocolate so they would know if someone replaced the chocolates with ones from the store. The students were told that the purpose of the study was to learn more about how people cope with "forbidden" foods. Next, students were randomly divided into three groups—one group received tips on coping by changing thoughts about eating; one was given lessons on acceptance; and the third group received no training. Students in the coping group learned ways to try to control cravings through distracting themselves or changing thoughts that came up around the need to eat the forbidden chocolate. In the acceptance group, students learned that trying to control urges to eat the chocolate wouldn't be helpful. Rather, they might notice their experience with mindfulness and willingness. The students who did not receive any training were simply told to try not to eat the chocolate. The acceptance training was associated with better outcomes for people who were most sensitive to intense food cravings.

The aim in practicing acceptance is to recognize that trying to control an unwanted experience is not helpful. Far better is an increased awareness around sensations and the willingness to sit with everything that may arise. Accepting food cravings includes not doing anything to directly control foods you encounter, and also not actively trying to experience urges less.

In crises, we face urges to seek quick fixes to change our mood. When you face urges, are you fighting, trying to think your way out, or giving in? Often people try to think their way out of cravings and rationalize indulging, or they mindlessly consume. Acceptance when urges arise requires less effort yet brings more benefit.

Accepting Setbacks

Failing to accept setbacks means facing more setbacks. G. Alan Marlatt coined the term *abstinence violation effect* to describe the way attributing a setback to some internal factor, such as something wrong with you beyond your control, and thinking of setbacks in all-or-nothing terms both lead to relapse (Marlatt and Gordon 1985). For example, if you decide that eating cake reflects your weakness, and if you consider a slice as sinful as a full cake, you are more likely to finish off the cake; you've really put yourself in a hopeless place. Alternatively, you may kindly notice that behaviors aren't all or none, then notice the ways you make sense of the action. You may notice that the cake looked really good and remind yourself that a bite is not a whole cake. Failing to accept your human fallibility and concluding that you are "out of control" can lead to giving up.

The abstinence violation effect nicely explains why the dieters we started this chapter with ate more ice cream and why eating may lead to more eating. If someone struggles with alcohol, has a drink, and decides that he is a failure and weak, he may drink more. Accepting setbacks and noticing thoughts is an alternative to holding rigid standards of self-discipline. Both self-soothing (as we will explore in the pages to come) and accepting your feelings, thoughts, and urges when you've slipped will help you take a step forward.

Accepting Hunger

Of course, depriving yourself of regular meals is unkind, unhelpful, and inconsistent with the message of this book. However, people often struggle with feeling afraid of experiencing any hunger. People may eat for emotional reasons due to fear of or unwillingness to accept the possibility of facing hunger. Many people who struggle with emotional eating perceive hunger in all-or-nothing terms, associating mild hunger with tremendous discomfort. The failure to accept hunger might maintain emotional eating. Judith Beck (2007) suggests purposely skipping a meal to keep track of the actual discomfort experienced rather than getting stuck in hypothetical, catastrophic fears.

However, if you are in the middle of overwhelming emotions, do not skip a meal if you can help it. If you are struggling with emotions and, for whatever reason, you are unable to get something to eat, you may at this point practice accepting hunger until food is available.

At times, I find myself booked for hours and hours with patients. I generally prefer to eat every few hours. However, when I am unable to eat due to a combination of poor planning and clinical duties, I find that accepting my feelings rather than either fighting or obsessing is more helpful in sitting with hunger and participating in the moment.

Costs and Benefits

In a crisis, as research reviewed earlier in the chapter points to, accepting both the costs and the benefits of a behavior is a challenge, as we tend to focus on the here and now rather than long-term goals. In practicing accepting both costs and benefits, you slow down to notice that any behavior you choose has pros and cons.

If you notice that you tend to pursue the same behavior repeatedly when you face intense emotions, you may consider writing out the benefits and costs of the behavior at a time when you are in a reasonable state of mind (Linehan 1993b). For example, a benefit of emotional eating might be distraction, while a cost might be extra calories. A benefit of sitting with emotions (not engaging in emotional eating) is building a sense of mastery, while a cost may be discomfort. It is helpful to specify whether a benefit or cost affects you in the short term or long term.

Exercise: Considering Costs and Benefits

Identify a *specific* behavior that you experience urges to engage in when you experience intense emotions, then list the benefits and costs of engaging in that behavior and of not engaging in that behavior. For example, you may list the benefits and costs of emotional eating and then the benefits and costs of sitting with emotions. Next to each benefit or cost, you may note an S if the effect of the behavior is short term, or an L if the behavior affects you in the long term.

♥

Soothing

One of the most helpful ways to stop engaging in mood-driven or impulsive behaviors is to thoughtfully soothe yourself in a strategic manner. In fact, one of the main tools to tolerate overwhelming distress is learning self-soothing (Linehan 1993a, 1993b). Thinking clearly while you feel strongly is a challenge. You may want to think about and productively plan soothing activities to cope ahead for a time when you may face overwhelming emotions. To soothe, you may need to do the opposite of feelings of engaging in impulse. Soothing is a step between emotion and emotional action that allows you to alleviate some distress without creating more problems.

In general, it's helpful to try to *soothe mindfully, one moment at a time.* If you immerse yourself in a warm bubble bath with burning candles on the rim of your tub and ruminate on your failures over the past decade, how helpful is that? When you face intense emotions, accepting the emotions moment to moment is the only way to cope well. Anticipating, "I'll feel this way forever," adds a lot of unjustified pain.

You may soothe by purposefully bringing your attention to naturally occurring pleasant events you may have overlooked. It's hard to relish the fun stuff when we are weighed down by emotions. After a stressful day, I noticed that a gym instructor played a song I loved years ago and hadn't heard in a while: hello, four minutes of bliss. (This example isn't especially notable, though it did entail my taking note.) A potential challenge we all face when we experience momentary joy involves wanting the event to last. Please play my song three more times! Oh no, it's coming to an end!

It's also important to soothe with a number of activities. If you planned a trip to Miami for a week, would you plan only to swim at the beach? What if it rains? Just as a trip may be most enjoyable when you consider a full scope of pleasures, so too practicing soothing with a range of options is effective. If you fear flying, and you rely on music and food to soothe, and as you take off the steward instructs you to turn off your music, and you didn't have time to purchase food at the airport, you may panic. Build a reservoir of options. Learn to soothe yourself with all your senses (Linehan 1993b).

Sound

Noticing sound diverts your attention from difficult emotions. You may notice sounds of nature, such as birds, wind, and rain. You may listen to a soothing voice or the sound of your own breath. Many people find listening to music a soothing activity. Music may calm, comfort, excite, or organize us. Music may even have therapeutic potential for people with a range of neurological conditions, animating people who struggle with Parkinson's disease and relaxing people disoriented by Alzheimer's or schizophrenia (Sacks 2007). When soothing through music, remember to select music that soothes rather than music that amplifies your current mood.

Sight

There are countless ways to move your focus away from suffering within to notice the soothing sights around you. You may consider looking at photographs of loved ones, noticing people around you, appreciating nature, or observing art or architecture. When I find myself on stalled subways, bringing attention to the people on the train relaxes me, while worrying and tensing increases my panic.

Touch

From the time we are born, touch is essential in soothing us; it even affects human development. Soothing yourself by massaging your hands or getting a massage, wearing soft, comfortable clothes, enjoying the sensation of a warm bath, applying lotion, playing with pets, rubbing sore muscles with a topical relaxant, holding a stress ball, feeling your feet grounded on the floor and your seat in your chair, placing a warm washcloth on your face—there are endless creative options. The website www.officeplay ground.com is one of many stress ball retailers. If you search the Internet, you'll find stress balls that emit an aromatherapy scent. Many of my clients who struggle with overwhelming emotions find that holding an ice cube as it melts provides a distraction from painful thoughts and urges. The ice may not feel soothing so much as it escorts your attention from your mind to present sensation—and that in itself may feel like a break.

Exercise: Frozen Orange

First, freeze an orange and leave it in the freezer until needed. Then, in a situation where you feel overwhelming emotions, if it's possible, start by noticing and labeling your emotions and their intensities as well as your urges, as described in the Noticing Intense Emotions exercise earlier in the chapter. Then, take the frozen orange in your hand.

1. How does the orange feel in your hand? You may notice the temperature and texture. You can squeeze it as you would squeeze a ball. You may notice the smell. What do you notice about its appearance?

2. If you notice your mind wander, can you return to the orange in your hand?

You may sit holding the orange for a few minutes and then pursue other ways to self-soothe, or notice whether your urges shift as you contact the present moment by attending to the orange with your full awareness.

♥

Taste

We all know that bringing our attention away from our minds to pleasant tastes may alleviate pain. We commonly soothe ourselves with comfort foods. Are there other ways to savor taste? You may simply notice flavor in a cup of tea. Personally, as I am writing, I am taking breaks to sip cinnamon spice tea. A flavorful ginger chew, mint, or kumquat may also be a subtle way to move your attention from your mind to your tongue. Which tastes can you think of that may bring you to the moment but don't lead to emotional eating?

Smell

Taking time to smell a scented candle, your favorite perfume, flowers, wood burning in the fireplace, aromatherapy oils, and other scents can ground you in the moment. Be aware, though, that some scents may exacerbate your pain. For example, you may notice that certain smells such as the cologne of a lost loved one or the scent of chocolate may move you toward sadness or intense urges. Can you think of scents that may be helpful to you?

Exercise: Scented Spa Towel

Soak a small towel or washcloth in a bowl of one cup cold water and two drops eucalyptus oil, then neatly roll the towel and place it in a resealable bag in your refrigerator.

1. In a time of difficult emotions when you seek comfort food in your refrigerator, notice and rate your emotions and urges, using the Noticing Intense Emotions exercise found earlier in this chapter.

2. Take out your towel and place it on your face.

3. While continuing to notice your emotions, bring your awareness to the sensation of the cold, scented towel on your face. Notice the feeling and the scent. Inhale deeply and exhale fully. You may place the towel on your forehead or toes or the back of your neck and bring your attention to breathing deeply as you notice any sensations.

4. After self-soothing with the towel, rate your current emotions and current urges. Did they increase? Decrease? Stay the same? Did self-soothing help you move away from engaging in any impulsive behaviors?

♥

Beyond soothing yourself with your senses, you may also cope with difficult feelings by getting active, eating wisely, seeking meaning, giving, cheerleading yourself, praying, and seeking support.

Get Active

Getting active can shift your attention away from entrapping thoughts. If you feel intense sadness and move your attention from thoughts about your worth to gardening or reading for a short period of time, your perspective may shift. Remember, changing your behavior changes your brain! Exercise you enjoy may serve as a fantastically meaningful activity if it falls under treating yourself kindly and taking a break from your mind.

Eat Wisely

Glucose provides fuel to your brain. Low blood glucose is linked to poor self-control, and restoring glucose to a sufficient level is one way to increase self-control (Gailliot and Baumeister 2007). Eating slowly and wisely when you face physiological hunger is an important step in coping with overwhelming emotions. If you know you will face a situation prompting strong feelings, you may pack a healthy snack to both reduce vulnerability caused by hunger and improve hunger-weakened self-control (Linehan 1993b).

Seek Meaning

Finding meaning in pain may facilitate acceptance and willingness (e.g., Linehan 1993b). If you frame pain as something you experience in the service of living according to your values rather than simply as pain, you may change your relationship with your experience. Moving away from emotional eating may not be a deprivation as much as an opportunity to live according to the path you choose.

All people experience a deep sense of imperfection. If I asked you to simply experience others noticing your flaws, you might feel quite distraught. If you are someone who deeply values relationships with others—including, perhaps, parenting—you may find meaning in your experience of pain as something that actually connects you—because it allows you to empathize with others, as we all feel imperfect at times. Would you be willing to sit with this sense that something is not completely right with you, so that when your child came home with this feeling, you'd really get it?

Finding meaning requires both mindfulness and flexible thinking. In *Man's Search for Meaning*, a powerful book on this topic, Viktor Frankl (1959) uses the example of a man mourning the unexpected death of his wife. In finding meaning for this tragedy, he noticed and accepted his pain. The widower appreciated that in his wife's dying first, she was spared outliving him, which would have caused *her* tremendous pain. Loving means losing. This widower, then, found meaning in seeing his loss as a contribution to his wife. She did not die alone and would therefore be spared the pain of widowhood. How have you found meaning in disappointing or painful experiences?

Give

Moving your attention from your pain to an awareness of others may serve as an opportunity to practice both mindfulness and meaningfully contributing to the lives of those around you (Linehan 1993b). If you face sadness over a job loss or simply feel depressed, noticing your sadness, accepting and acknowledging your feelings, and giving yourself permission to bring your attention outside yourself to someone else may not make you feel better, but it may help you live bigger. You cultivate a more expansive awareness.

A psychologist I adore struggled with heroin abuse and suicidal thoughts earlier in his life. He recalls that the only job he could find was bathing people with developmental disabilities. At the time, he thought of himself from a narrow vantage point, believing his being alive was causing people pain. In bathing others, he could shift his awareness from what was wrong with him to this other person, and this moment, rather than his own painful emotional conclusions. In a moment of bathing a person mindfully, he accepted his pain and for the first time saw he could actually live in a way that mattered (K. Wilson 2010):

> I spent so many years dead certain that I was a drain on the universe. Getting near me would wear you out and cause you damage. The closer you got, the more damage you would take. Mostly people did not realize it until it was too late, but eventually they always did. That was the story I inhabited...

But there on my knees, in that steamy bathroom, I found myself useful. I did not know that I could be useful. And, I cannot express how much it meant to me on that day, in that bathroom, on my knees, finding myself useful. And, now, remembering it all, my eyes fill with tears of gratitude.

It's helpful to remember that, in giving, you're not minimizing your pain or judging yourself or others. You are expanding your focus and getting out of minding and into living.

Cheerlead

Remember, distress tolerance relates to your *perception* of your ability to cope with distress. When emotions overwhelm you, notice distressing thoughts, and kindly support yourself the way you might offer support to someone else you care about. A wise client of mine noticed reminding herself after twenty years of struggling with obesity and continuing to try new programs and diets that saying "I don't give up" is a fantastic alternative to getting caught in "I've tried everything" or "Nothing works." You may also cheer yourself along by bringing awareness to times you struggled and coped well (Linehan 1993b). The point isn't to develop false confidence or replace "bad" thoughts with "good" ones. This is about cultivating an environment that is helpful to moving forward according to what you value. You may think of a couple of inspiring quotes or phrases such as "Breathe deeply and live fully" and "One moment at a time." I love Eleanor Roosevelt's recommendation, "Do one thing every day that scares you."

Pray

Taking a moment to open your heart to pray to a higher power can facilitate coping (Linehan 1993b). And you need not subscribe to a particular faith to do it: the wise psychologist mentioned above, Kelly Wilson, describes himself as an atheist who prays. Any prayer consistent with acceptance is helpful. You're not praying for pain to go away; rather, you may pray for the courage to accept or connect with truth or wisdom.

Prayer may promote healing in a time of suffering. Through the practice of prayer, you may develop faith that possibility exists. Prayer provides a sense that you are not alone—you are connected either with the divine or with a wise place within. When despair creeps up, prayer illuminates.

In a time of distress, you may pray for others who struggle, shifting your focus away from yourself to attend to another, which might feel quite meaningful. Praying for another synthesizes the skill of giving with the practice of praying. In times of distress, remembering that you are part of a shared humanity feels comforting. There have been times I have felt alone in my pain, and when I brought to mind and considered others similarly struggling, and I devoted attention to wishing them freedom from suffering, I noticed myself feeling both more connected and less caught in my perception of my own pain.

Seek Support

Social support is a huge buffer against stress and can be quite powerful in a time of pain. You may gather support by calling a friend, meeting with a psychologist, attending a support group, calling a helpline, listening to messages on your voicemail from people you care about, or thinking about people you care about. Of course, certain "supports" may exacerbate stress. Consider what sorts of support may feel most helpful in your specific situation. We'll spend more time on relationships in the next chapter.

Preparing a Graceful Plan for Soothing

As we all know, coping when emotions engulf us can feel impossible. Doing what you can now in preparation for the time when emotions and urges feel overpowering will increase your ability to cope well.

You may start by thinking about collecting mementos to keep with you that will help you access mindfulness and wisdom as you move through the day. You may also prepare similar reminders that you keep in your home. You may prepare different coping plans depending on the emotional experience, as you may cope with urges to eat and with feelings of profound fear differently. Collectively, these meaningful objects, spaces, and practices of using them are called *soothing savers*.

Claudia carried with her a small toiletry case to help her with emotional eating. Inside were a couple of important photos, several inspiring quotes, a meditation bracelet, a list of the pros and cons of emotional eating, a small laminated pie chart of her values (which we will review in chapter 9), a pleasing scent, a strong mint, a low-sugar granola bar for physical hunger, and a list of alternative activities she finds helpful. She also created a list of inspiring songs to listen to while breathing. At home, when she felt urges to eat for emotional reasons, she went to a corner she had set up in her home office where she had a comfy chair, a small desktop fountain to watch and listen to, a display of greeting cards she had saved, a whiteboard she used for her gratitude list to challenge her sense of deprivation, a list of helpful activities to pursue at home, and another list of costs and benefits around ordering take-out.

Each of us is unique in what we find soothing. For this technique to be helpful, your reminders to accept and soothe rather than fight and act impulsively need to be specific to you.

Exercise: Gathering Soothing Savers

Spend some time identifying situations likely to cause mood-driven behavior. You will need a number of index cards.

1. Identify at least two particular emotions or urges that you aim to cope better with in the situations you are thinking of.

2. For each emotion or urge you identified, create a set of eleven index cards. At the top of each index card, label the emotion or describe the urge. You will dedicate one card to each of the following categories:

   a. My ways to practice mindfulness

   b. My ways to eat wisely

   c. My ways to soothe with sounds

   d. My ways to soothe with sight

e. My ways to soothe with taste

f. My ways to soothe with smell

g. My ways to cheerlead

h. My ways to pray

i. My ways to notice meaning

j. My ways to practice giving

k. My supports

On each card, list several category-specific practices that you are willing to try in order to cope with the emotion or urge. Create separate sets of index cards for each emotion or urge, because what you find helpful in dealing with food cravings may differ from what you find helpful in coping with intense fear, for example.

3. Highlight several practices from your lists that you will commit to using this week. You may even start by practicing on a less intense emotional experience to get in the habit.

4. After using a practice, notice whether it helped you align yourself with acceptance and commitment to what you care about.

5. Modify your lists as necessary, so that they contain the most helpful and effective practices.

6. Now prepare a final list for each situation you've identified.

Remember that the purpose of soothing savers is not to feel better—it's to live better. You may actually *feel* better when you overeat. Compared to overeating or other unhealthy coping methods, these soothing savers have a potentially lower payoff in the short term. Yet over time, practicing using them may help you find freedom in a range of options.

♥

Summary

This chapter explored ways our strong emotions can affect our behaviors, including how bad moods may veer us away from the path that matters to us. This occurs both because emotions can get in the way of clear thinking and because not accepting our emotions may lead to impulsive behaviors. Learning to mindfully accept our emotions, urges, and setbacks while also soothing ourselves in an adaptive way can allow us to gracefully face temptations ranging from the ice cream buffet to the fleeting desire to abandon an important aspiration.

Chapter 8

CULTIVATING
SELF-COMPASSION

Compassion is probably the only antitoxin of the soul; where there is compassion even the most poisonous impulses remain relatively harmless.

—ERIC HOFFER

I love research on parenting, because what we know about what helps us raise children who are able to manage emotions, play well with others, and pursue meaningful activities provides us with rich information on how to develop ourselves.

In considering the most helpful way to raise a child or, for our purposes, to advance yourself, consider the following choices.

1. Low on expectations, high on warmth

2. Low on expectations, low on warmth

3. High on expectations, high on warmth

4. High on expectations, low on warmth

You may think about expectation as what you aim for and warmth as how much you accept and understand your experience and emotions throughout the process. For example, low expectations and high warmth may mean you don't push yourself and understand that you need to take it easy. High expectations and low warmth may look like a coach interacting with an athlete mid-game: "I don't care what it takes. WIN!"

Which of the choices listed above most reflects your style in dealing with yourself? Do you have a sense of which approach works best? Take a moment to think about your experience: you may reflect on people you've learned from, which of these stances they embody, and which fostered achievement in you. Research indicates that choice 3—the combination of setting aspirational goals (high expectations) and also attending to your experience with kindness (high warmth)—relates most strongly to mastery (Baumrind 1971).

Simultaneously aiming to excel and understanding that you are human exemplifies self-compassion. By contrast, assuming that you won't succeed and lowering your expectations is neither considerate nor kind—these can be thoughts to notice mindfully, but not to act on. High standards don't relate to suffering; self-critical judgments do. Self-criticism, more than perfectionism, relates to anxiety, depression, and eating disorder symptoms (Dunkley et al. 2006). There is such a difference between when you pursue a task chaperoned by self-acceptance and when you decide that your performance defines you. A challenge we all face involves maintaining our equanimity in the face of pursuits that matter.

If you struggle with emotional eating, you may try to plan your meals, eat mindfully, and also accept your emotions and setbacks. You may notice wisely, "I'll do my best to sit with emotions and eat right—and I'll never wear a size 2, given my body type." Or, "It makes sense I ate an unplanned snack given that this is a tough habit to break. I will also make sure to slow down the next time I face urges." This is quite different from the harsh "I overate, I need to skip a meal"; the permissive "It's okay, I'll change when things are easier"; or the passive "Why bother?"

Life is hard. When you face a setback such as eating for emotional reasons, receiving negative feedback, gaining weight, or experiencing the painful end of a relationship, do you judge yourself harshly, experience shame, or give up? All too often, when circumstances challenge our core, we get critical and rely on donuts, drugs, or dear friends. Honing your own capacity to comfort yourself will provide you with enduring benefits. As discussed in previous chapters, getting critical, drowning in shame, or not accepting that you are human are all habits of mind that get you more stuck. Self-compassion nourishes you, protecting you against emotional distress and promoting your health.

What Is Self-Compassion?

Self-compassion entails "being open to and moved by one's own suffering, experiencing feelings of caring and kindness toward oneself, taking an understanding, nonjudgmental attitude toward one's inadequacies and failures, and recognizing that one's experience is part of the common human experience" (Neff 2003, 224).

To break this down, self-compassion includes:

1. Practicing self-kindness and understanding

2. Seeing your experience as part of being human

3. Noticing your thoughts and feelings mindfully

All of these processes relate to one another and fall under the broader category of mindfulness and acceptance. While we have talked about acceptance in the context of accepting our circumstances, in practicing self-compassion, we direct acceptance toward ourselves. When you practice self-compassion, you understand and accept your setbacks and yourself. You notice that, as a person like all other humans, you are not perfect and you experience life's challenges. Self-compassion is valuable in itself, and it's like currency—you can use it to acquire other valuable things. For example, self-compassion both builds on the skills covered in this book, including mindfulness, emotion regulation, and distress tolerance, and serves as the basis for those skills.

I would venture to guess that you and every person you know share the human experience of feeling there is something not quite right with you. You can change your relationship with this experience by noticing that it is so human, so universal. In lectures attended by psychologists, when the audience is asked whether they have the experience of feeling uncomfortably flawed, every person raises a hand. And I doubt this is just a problem among psychologists. This awareness of shared human experience can connect you with others.

When you practice providing yourself with warmth, you create responses within yourself that resemble those activated by a soothing other (Gilbert 2009). When we activate self-compassion, our soothing system starts operating, which can feel more useful than getting stuck in guilt and self-incriminating thoughts.

Annabelle's Story

For most of her life, Annabelle struggled with negative judgments about her body. She worried a lot about dating and spent years avoiding dating entirely. The thought of making herself vulnerable by facing judgments from a potential romantic partner seemed intolerable. After a brief relationship that ended painfully ten years ago, she decided to stop dating. Occasionally, she tried to meet new people, but she found herself stuck in thinking that no one could love her and blaming herself when she did not hear back from others. "I'm not good enough, or pretty, and I've heard it's impossible to meet someone after forty," she concluded.

If she did go on a date, she censored herself and would never make any requests, believing this might jeopardize her chances. After a couple of first dates that didn't turn into seconds, she decided to put off dating until she lost thirty pounds. After learning about radical acceptance, Annabelle proudly announced that she now used the skill of acceptance to soothe her pain around the idea that she would never find a partner. I clarified that acceptance relates to kindness, and of course you may accept that you are single, but what Annabelle labeled "acceptance" was truly hopelessness.

We talked about how compassion is so different from giving up, and we worked on noticing the desire to give up. Caring about yourself means you allow yourself to feel what you feel and want what you want rather than drowning in shame and letting go of what matters to you. So many people struggle with insecurities around dating, especially when dating experiences have felt painful.

In therapy, Annabelle and I spent time moving away from the particulars of her situation to consider how she might respond if her niece and goddaughter, Cara, shared the same struggle. Annabelle told me Cara was shy and felt insecure around her high school peers; she didn't feel as smart or as popular. "Of course I'd encourage her to go to her prom," Annabelle said emphatically. We noticed the discrepancies between how she treats herself and her approach to Cara.

Annabelle acknowledged her pain around feeling lonely and also acknowledged that wanting a companion was not selfish or demanding, but human. We created a plan to bring kindness to her experience, both accepting her current single status and also initiating contact with people who seemed interesting. She learned to cheer herself on and also to notice thoughts that got in the way of her treating herself with compassion. It helped her to bring herself back to the values she would impart to Cara.

She also practiced bringing the same kindness and understanding to herself around eating. When she ate a "forbidden" food, she acknowledged her slip with acceptance and soothingly coached herself to continue toward her goal. Eventually, she realized that marking foods as forbidden was cruel, and she allowed herself to taste in moderation the foods everyone craves. She noticed that she actually ate less when she gave herself permission.

While dating and sitting with feelings take effort, Annabelle noticed that she felt energized by her new approach and concluded that even if she neither met "the one" nor lost the thirty pounds, she would accomplish something meaningful by treating herself well.

Self-Compassion vs. Self-Esteem

Self-compassion and self-esteem differ. A fundamental difference is that judgments generate self-esteem, while self-compassion reflects acceptance. Generally, we obtain high self-esteem by succeeding. Our self-worth depends on our success. To decide, "I'm great" or "I'm better than most," you judge—and judging yourself, albeit favorably, simply sharpens the skill of judging. This makes you susceptible to negative judgments. As soon as you earn praise, you may find yourself struggling to retain the temporary honor. You work hard to win, only to then work harder to defend the championship. Implicitly, if you need to be "better than" to be worthwhile, you maintain the core belief that you are not good enough as you are.

You may do all sorts of stuff to pump up your self-esteem, and you may in fact improve your self-esteem. But the side effects of trying to build self-esteem include being self-absorbed and alone, as well as facing more emotional and physical problems (e.g., Crocker and Park 2004). Needing to feel a certain way about yourself can create a lot of stress and not really increase your achievement. If your self-esteem is on the line, you may drop a goal in order to avoid losing your good feelings about yourself. This limits your opportunities to learn and master new tasks. Additionally, when your self-esteem is in jeopardy, you may feel overwhelmed and cope by overeating (Tice and Bratslavsky 2000).

Self-compassion can provide some of the positive feelings associated with self-esteem without the side effects. Self-esteem is like pumping yourself up with helium—you get bigger, but not in substance; instead you are more vulnerable to a loud and painful pop when your self-esteem is pierced. Self-compassion is more substantive and authentic.

The Science of Self-Compassion

Often, the idea of self-compassion is received as something that "sounds nice" but is "too touchy-feely." For a moment, notice thoughts that come up around practicing self-compassion. What are your thoughts? Do you believe any of the following?

- Treating myself kindly will make me lazy and/or selfish.

- Being tough is what keeps me in line.

- Treating myself kindly leads to indulging (e.g., overeating).

- Given my history, I won't be able to do this.

I find it thought-provoking that presenting as "self-deprecating" is a virtue associated with modesty, while the practice of loving-kindness or self-compassion may engender judgments. So often, in our minds, personal growth relates to competition, consequence, and criticism, while we associate self-compassion with indulgence. Now that you are aware of your thoughts around the practice of self-compassion, let's explore some facts that may relate to your concerns.

Interestingly, self-compassion, not self-condemnation, cultivates change. Each operates in a self-reinforcing cycle.

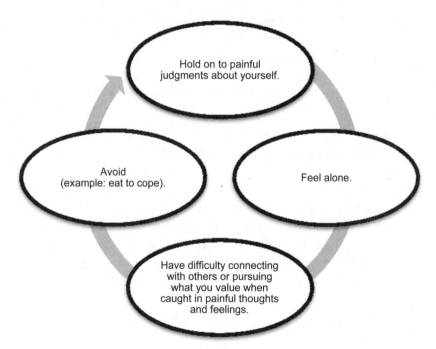

Figure 6: The Self-Critical Cycle

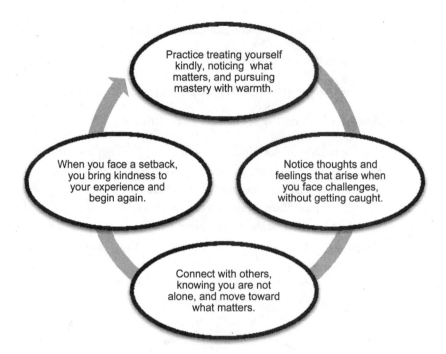

Figure 7: The Self-Compassionate Cycle

Self-compassion actually improves your ability to manage emotions and urges. Self-compassion changes the way you cope with distress. People with more self-compassion ruminate less and experience more positive emotions than people low in self-compassion. When you face a setback or a negative event, if you respond with self-compassion, you tend to be more able to accept your behavior without feeling overwhelmed (Leary et al. 2007). A lot of this may sound familiar if you think about some of the examples from chapter 7 on coping with pain without a second helping. It's easier to both learn and move forward when you accept that slipping is human and that your setbacks do not define you.

Self-Compassion and Mastery

Let's say you struggle with a serious smoking addiction and depend on nicotine physically and emotionally. What might be helpful in quitting? Popular strategies include listening to scary pep talks replete with photographs of diseased lungs, methodically keeping track of your smoking to cut back strategically, applying nicotine patches, and engaging in hypnosis. Notice that those strategies suggest that you need to get busy and take action and change. Interestingly, practicing accepting yourself actually facilitates change in smokers. People who struggled with smoking addiction who were taught to practice self-compassion reduced their smoking more quickly than groups using other well-established smoking cessation techniques, even when they felt less ready to change smoking habits and felt critical of themselves (Kelly et al. 2010). Similarly, when students who did not perform well on exams practiced self-compassion, they were more able to access acceptance and emotion regulation and move toward mastery. In other words, self-compassion is one of the best ways to zap avoidance and unnecessary distress (Neff, Hsieh, and Dejitterat 2005). The idea of studying while stuck in negative thoughts seems unhelpful, while self-compassion fosters the mindfulness necessary to pursue tasks you might ordinarily wish to avoid.

Self-Compassion and Eating

We all know that comfort foods like macaroni and cheese, home fries, and matzo ball soup soothe. As we've explored in earlier chapters, and as you well know from your experience, comfort from food is fleeting. Relying on food means depending on something outside you for coziness. If eating serves you as an escape from negative emotions, self-compassion is a viable form of awareness. You may access ease at any time without depending on a temporary external fix, though this source of comfort will take skill and practice.

In one study, researchers studied the tendency to restrict and feel guilty about eating in a group of nearly 100 women in college. The researchers explained that the study would look at eating and television watching. Each woman received a donut, and after eating the donut, each woman was asked to taste-test candy. As you may recall from chapter 7, people often feel inclined to overeat in response to breaking a diet rule. Before the study, researchers compassionately told a group of randomly selected women, "Everyone eats unhealthily sometimes, and everyone in this study eats this stuff, so I don't think there's any reason to feel really bad about it." Women who were provided with the compassionate explanation before the study did not eat more during the taste test, even if they were dieting (Adams and Leary 2007). Compassion reduced distress and led to improved eating. In other words, when you practice acceptance, you are more able to get back on track.

Self-compassion means you forgive yourself. When you feel guilty about eating, that often leads to more eating.

Exercise: Creating a Compassionate Coach

Often it is challenging to cultivate self-compassion. It may be helpful to bring to mind an image of a compassionate other to help you experience self-compassion.

1. Spend a few moments bringing to mind an image of a compassionate person. It may be a person you know, such as a grandparent, teacher, or friend. Or it may be someone you don't know personally.

2. Once you have selected a person who really epitomizes kindness in your mind, attend to certain details of this person: in your mind, notice his or her countenance, appearance, voice, and posture.

3. How do you feel as you sit with this person in your mind?

4. Now, write a supportive letter to yourself from the perspective of the compassionate person. What might he or she say to you when you face a challenge? You may choose a specific challenge, such as eating for emotional reasons or feeling anxious. What would this person say or do upon seeing your struggle? After you write this letter, read it aloud in a compassionate tone.

5. When you next face an urge or difficulty, visualize this image—the warmth, the understanding, the strength. Then, act toward yourself the way the compassionate person would

act toward you. This may entail saying something he or she might say to you, rereading the letter, or embodying a supportive posture by rubbing your shoulders.

6. Allow yourself to really experience the compassion.

7. In practicing self-compassion, notice if self-critical thoughts come up, and use them as an opportunity to return to compassion.

(Adapted from Gilbert 2009)

♥

Self-Compassion vs. Self-Absorption

Sharon Salzberg (2005, 17) explains that using the language of "'I, me, and mine' isn't the same as loving ourselves, just as shallow martyrdom where we only think of others and never care about ourselves isn't really generosity, because both are coming from the same wrong intention. Loving ourselves points us to capacities of resilience, compassion, and understanding within that are simply part of being alive."

Self-Compassion Paves the Way for Closeness

Directing kindness toward yourself may provide enduring comfort and also facilitate closeness with others. When you practice treating yourself with ease, gentleness, and validation, these manners develop, and you may apply this kindness toward others, helping build meaningful, lasting relationships. Self-compassion relates to healthy relationships (Neff 2006). Honing the capacity to treat yourself with understanding can facilitate your ability to give to and understand others. It's hard to contribute to meaningful relationships if you feel depleted and emotionally exhausted.

It bears repeating that if you wonder whether these practices work, you need to experiment with them over time. To begin exploring self-compassion and connecting with others, you may participate in the mindfulness practice below. When you direct attention and kindness toward yourself and others, you don't need to force love. You are simply bringing awareness. If the term "loving-kindness" feels overwhelming or not right, you may replace it with "kind interest."

You may practice the exercise either in a mindful seated posture (spine upright, eyes focused on a point or closed, feet flat on the floor or legs crossed comfortably in a lotus position). You may also practice loving-kindness as you walk. As you walk, you may notice your steps and also direct your attention to the practice. Often, when we walk, our minds run elsewhere.

I learned this practice from Sharon Salzberg, who adapted it from her teacher in Burma. Sharon practices loving-kindness whenever she is waiting or traveling. Imagine if waiting no longer meant losing time, but producing love and regulating your emotions. When you speak with Sharon, loving-kindness emanates from her. The benefits of practicing loving-kindness are supported by science. Neuroimaging studies find that loving-kindness enhances our ability to manage our emotions, especially during times of distress, and also increases our empathic response to another's distress (Lutz et al. 2008).

I've noticed that when I practice bringing awareness to people I may not usually think about (the operator who calls me when I receive an emergency page from a patient, the unseen person who delivers my packages, the grocer, the bank teller), I accumulate positive emotions and build mastery in my level of connectedness. I also create a sense of community, which I value.

Exercise: Mindfulness Practice— Loving-kindness for All

1. When you are ready to begin, offer kindness to yourself by silently repeating: "May I be safe. May I be happy. May I be healthy. May I live with ease."

2. Continue to repeat each phrase with awareness, at a pace that feels gentle, and in a tone that embodies compassion.

3. When thoughts and feelings arise, notice them and return to your ever-present guide, your breath. Then refocus your attention on the phrases of loving-kindness toward yourself.

4. After several minutes, bring to your awareness the image of a person who has helped you or inspired you. Spend several minutes allowing this person's image to exist in your awareness and offering this person the phrases of loving-kindness ("May he be safe," etc.).

5. Next, bring to mind a person you know who struggles or faces a challenge. This may be anyone from a store clerk to someone you recognize from your commute to a close friend. Bring your awareness to offering this person phrases of loving-kindness for several minutes with your full attention. When your mind wanders, you may reorient your attention by focusing on each word.

6. Last, bring your attention to a person you find difficult. Not the person you hate the most, but someone moderately difficult. Offer this person loving-kindness as your face and body remain relaxed.

7. Return to your breath for several minutes, again directing the phrases of loving-kindness toward yourself.

♥

If you practice self-compassion, you may notice that you create metaphoric space in your heart, making room for yourself and others. Again, the practice is not about forcing kindness; it's about bringing attention. At times, when we focus our attention and change the way we attend to it, our ability to be aware of the goodness in the moment expands.

Self-Criticism and Connection

Self-criticism may get in the way of close connections and leave you vulnerable to relying on food for comfort. It's hard to imagine opening yourself up to connect with others when self-criticism seeps through you. If you are caught up in critical thoughts, it's hard to really hear someone else and pay attention to them. Self-critical thoughts, like replaying your eating setbacks, distract and capture our attention, interfering with our ability to connect with others. Often, my patients who struggle with shame around eating or anxiety in social situations report that people perceive them as cold or aloof. Knowing them, I know that, like Annabelle, these people value relationships highly and want to get close, but getting caught in self-critical thoughts can get in the way of their connecting.

Perceptions of rejection can lead to self-isolation and eating for emotional reasons. If you notice the thought that others don't like you—or in fact another person dislikes you—you will not live better if you are unnecessarily tough on yourself.

If you struggle to treat yourself with understanding, you may feel overly dependent on others for reassurance and support. Relying on someone to carry you differs from asking someone to hold your hand. We all cherish compassion from others. Exclusively relying on someone else to provide you with support may overwhelm the other person and also not fully meet your needs.

Kelly's Story

Kelly is thin, and she struggles with binge eating when she feels fat. She described to me a recent bingeing episode that was triggered when she was with a group of friends waiting outside a hip new nightclub. As her group waited anxiously to go in, the bouncer allowed only her friend Nicole inside. Kelly was sure the only reason Nicole was invited to party had to do with her being "the skinniest." Kelly felt ashamed by her appearance and ended up bingeing later that night after concluding, "I'm lame." My humble thought about the night was that Kelly wasn't admitted because she was underage. Regardless, even if it had to do with her appearance, her judgment, more than the facts at hand, resulted in her emotional eating and also her decision to distance herself from Nicole. In therapy, we focused on gaining perspective about negative judgments and bringing awareness to the habit of taking such judgments personally. In addition to moving away from the fog of her thinking, Kelly learned to use such a situation as an opportunity to practice self-compassion.

Exercise: Learning Self-Compassion to Face Self-Critical Thoughts

Often, self-critical thoughts can feel like facts, or we might simply experience them so often that it's hard to notice they are there— they're like a sound you fail to notice because you're habituated to it. In this exercise, you will bring mindful awareness to self-critical thoughts and learn to practice self-soothing with words intended to replace your inner critic with a compassionate voice. If writing is helpful, use your notebook.

1. Notice a self-critical thought that arises often.

2. Add kindness. You may offer kindness to yourself by wishing yourself compassion in a tone and demeanor that reflects kindness. Choose a phrase that resonates—create your own or use one from the mindful loving-kindness practice earlier in this chapter.

3. As you offer yourself kindness, do so mindfully with your full attention on the words and practice. What do you notice?

♥

On a personal note, several months ago, I attended a large event alone. Going to this celebration reflected my values, but it was not easy logistically or emotionally. I found myself approaching the party stumbling in my heels and getting stuck in worries. I practiced turning my attention to phrases of loving-kindness such as "May I be at ease" and "May I be filled with loving-kindness." Moving my attention to the words, adopting a slow deliberate breath, and relaxing my face into a half-smile reminded me of why I was there and helped me actually participate fully without getting stuck in self-critical thoughts that had the effect of punishing me for living according to what I value.

Self-Compassion and Asking for What You Want

You may treat yourself kindly by asking others clearly for what you want. Interpersonal effectiveness and asking directly for what you want are core DBT skills that facilitate managing emotions and building a life that matters (Linehan 1993a, 1993b). So often, people who are self-critical or believe from past experience that others can't be trusted may struggle with assertiveness. If you find yourself caught in thinking that you are not worthy or worrying a lot about what others may think, it makes a lot of sense that it would feel challenging to clearly ask someone for something that you want. Asking clearly for what you want in a respectful way will not only help you—it will also improve your relationships. Many people notice that not asking for what you want clearly leads to distance in a relationship or to eventually feeling frustrated and blowing up.

Think back for a moment to the case of Annabelle. Annabelle truly believed that if she asked for anything, she would burden someone. She didn't ask her friends to fix her up on dates, thinking they'd feel annoyed and wouldn't know what to say. She also had a very hard time telling men she met that she had certain dietary restrictions. Since Annabelle saw herself as not worthy, she acted as though anything she needed was too much. Eventually, after she had done a good amount of work on acceptance and self-compassion, she asked her friend Sarah about fixing her up, describing her situation, feelings, and request candidly, without apologizing. She said something like, "Sarah, I've been thinking I'd like to date and I know you know many people. I would love to meet one of Robert's friends since Robert seems to surround himself with smart guys. Can you ask him if he knows of anyone I may like? I hope at some point we could all go on a double date!"

Annabelle felt anxious approaching Sarah with this request. But in making the approach, she practiced self-compassion, mindfulness, and opposite action, choosing to see the request as an opportunity to build mastery. And Sarah and Annabelle grew closer by connecting over dating—the opposite of what Annabelle had feared would happen if she asked for anything from a friend. Annabelle also was able to tell a date about her dietary restrictions. She enjoyed herself more in a restaurant she felt comfortable ordering in, and while the date wasn't perfect, she felt less anxious and more able to focus on the conversation. She found that dating with self-compassion felt like a hobby, while dating with self-criticism reminded her of interviewing for a job.

As social beings, we understandably need to (and want to) rely on others from time to time. If you notice thoughts that you are not deserving, practicing asking for something may serve as both a practice in self-compassion and a practice in improving your relationships. If assertiveness feels like a challenge, grab your notebook and prepare to practice this skill using the following exercise.

Exercise: Treating Yourself Kindly by Asking for What You Want Clearly

1. Bring to mind a situation where you find yourself struggling to make a request. This may range from asking a café in your neighborhood to offer soymilk to asking a person in your life for something big. What is it that you want? Choose a situation that seems important but not overwhelming.

2. How might making this request build your self-compassion?

3. You may practice coping ahead by jotting down the specifics of how you will assert yourself. Ask yourself:

    a. How may I present the *facts* of the situation?

    b. How may I share my *feelings* appropriately?

    c. How may I state clearly what I'm *asking*?

    d. How may I offer some word of *appreciation* or reward for fulfilling my request to increase the likelihood the person I ask will oblige?

4. As you prepare to make the request or cope with the response, practice self-compassion by practicing mindfulness and self-validation. What might this look and sound like?

♥

Many people who struggle with eating have a difficult time asking clearly for what matters, and this in turn has an impact on relationships. Improving relationships, both with others and with yourself, relates to improving your eating (e.g., Rieger et al. 2010). Learning to make requests and developing self-compassion are tools in improving relationships, and both take practice. Remember the idea of combining high demands and high warmth. The goal in practicing asking for what you want is not necessarily to get what you want (though that's always nice) but to treat yourself with kindness.

Self-Compassion vs. Reassurance Seeking

Often, when you obsess over eating or your weight, it's tempting to ask others for feedback on whether you've lost or gained weight. It can also feel natural to worry about any comment on your appearance—for example, noticing that the last time you saw someone she said you looked good, but today she said nothing. Both asking for a lot of feedback on your appearance and scrutinizing others' comments may get in the way of treating yourself kindly. If someone often comments about your appearance or eating in a way that isn't helpful, this may be an opportunity to practice asking for what you want—for them to stop this sort of commentary. Before you decide to make such a request, consider whether this would reflect an act of self-compassion or would improve the relationship. Alternatively, you may bring kindness toward yourself by noticing your urges to ruminate on others' comments or on your own urges to ask, then letting go of these habits by choosing to participate in the moment.

Summary

As you well know, you can't change your past or your parents, but you can modify the way you treat yourself to affect your present experience. This chapter highlights how self-kindness can pave the way for connecting, managing emotions, and improving eating. Expecting either too much or too little of yourself is not kind. Neither is treating yourself indulgently or restrictively.

There is an idea in Judaism that I love. Sages explain that by forgiving someone wholeheartedly, you atone for your own sins and amass the other person's virtues. Regardless of your faith, you may notice that when you forgive both yourself and others, you let go of affliction and open yourself up to blessing. In the words of Pema Chödrön (1994, 128), "When you begin to touch your heart or let your heart be touched, you begin to discover that it's bottomless, that it doesn't have any resolution, that this heart is huge, vast, and limitless."

Chapter 9

TASTING VALUES

Your time is limited, so don't waste it living someone else's
life. Don't be trapped by dogma—which is living with the
results of other people's thinking. Don't let the noise of
others' opinions drown out your own inner voice. And most
important, have the courage to follow your heart and
intuition. They somehow already know what you truly want
to become. Everything else is secondary.

—STEVE JOBS

There is a Zen story about a man riding a horse at a gallop down the
road. An observer on the road shouts, "Where are you going?"
and the rider replies, "I don't know, ask the horse!" (Thich Nhat
Hanh 1998). Not knowing what matters to you can create a lot of chaos,
like driving in traffic and heavy rain with no destination in mind.

My client Reed decided at a young age he wanted to work as an attorney in legal aid. He pursued internships and volunteered in ways that
would build his resume for law school admission. He worked after college
as a paralegal and studied intensely for the LSAT. But there was something about Reed's enthusiasm about this career course that seemed inauthentic. At times, I felt he was trying to convince me, and he seemed

uncomfortably anxious. Eventually, he noticed he didn't want to be a lawyer. He wasn't sure how it was that he had come to believe he did want it; he thought it had a bit to do with others encouraging him from a young age and also his own actions—he really acted the part of an aspiring lawyer. It felt uncomfortable for him to sit with the realization that law was no longer a career goal.

In our own ways, we all struggle with falling into goals, habits, and stories that may not actually really matter to us. We find solace in their familiarity. We may feel unclear about what really matters to us. Initially, it feels comfortable to hold on to familiar beliefs, behaviors, and feelings. Our familiar perceptions of ourselves give us a sense of coherence and predictability. Social psychologists notice that people are motivated to make their behaviors conform to their views of themselves. According to *self-verification theory*, our allegiance to our stories about ourselves is quite powerful (Swann 1983).

Rather than mindlessly fall into traps of untruth and routine, in this chapter you will notice the ways food and weight direct your energy, and you will bring awareness and activity to the life directions you value.

The Effects of Eating on Self-Worth

We all judge ourselves according to certain criteria, such as how we perform in our careers, our friendships, our reputations, and even our possessions. For a moment, think about how you judge yourself. What are your criteria? One of the core features of an unhealthy relationship with eating includes spending a lot of time preoccupied with controlling shape and weight (Fairburn 2008).

Often, when something bothers us, the topic captivates our attention. When you are in a dispute with someone, it may seize your attention for hours or even years. In a similar way, when we struggle with ourselves and obsess about what we want to eat, will eat, or did eat, attending to other aspects in life can feel challenging.

Exercise: How Do I Judge Myself?

We all evaluate ourselves. If you notice that you tend to feel good or bad based on how you are doing in certain realms, that provides information that you really care about these areas of your life. In this exercise (based on Fairburn 2008), grab your notebook and bring awareness to the criteria you use to evaluate yourself.

1. List areas or criteria that matter to you. You do not need to rank how you are doing. Just list what matters. You also do not need to represent what you'd like to have matter to you, only what you observe actually matters.

2. Now, imagine that you could represent your life in terms of a pie chart. Place the factors you listed above in a pie chart and represent each factor in a way that symbolizes its relative importance in your life now. For example, if you listed relationships with friends and family, and you feel that symbolizes one-third of what matters to you now, label one-third of the pie to reflect that.

3. Now, list areas that you would like to matter in your life.

4. Make a new pie chart that reflects how you aspire to live your life.

5. What are the differences between the current pie chart and your ideal pie chart?

♥

In the preceding exercise, what percentage of each pie represents eating, appearance, or weight? For many people, eating becomes the focus of life rather than simply an aspect of life, as the pie chart on the next page reflects (Fairburn 2008).

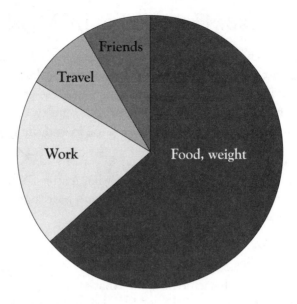

Figure 8: Life Pie

Focusing a lot of attention on food and shape not only is symptomatic of problems with eating, but also maintains a problematic relationship with food and your shape. Ruminating about eating means losing the moment and suffering more.

The Cost of Overvaluing

If your appearance really matters to you and you feel trapped by food, it makes sense you would spend a lot of your energy absorbed by those areas. Our society, especially the advertising industry, encourages us to make food, weight, and appearance a central focus. Let's explore mindfully what the consequences are.

Overvaluing the body leads us to undervalue other areas in life. Is it helpful to have a pie where one slice is much bigger than the others? It's like putting all of your savings into a single, risky investment. If your worth depends on how you look and what you eat, and you are struggling with emotional eating and your self-image, how effective is it to make the focus of your life the area that causes you pain? Making eating and your appearance the focus of your life will perpetuate your struggle.

For example, if your self-worth depends on your children's successes, and they aren't doing well, you will suffer more because their accomplishments and failures define you. Making your self-worth dependent on their successes may also lead you to place unnecessary pressure on them, which may negatively affect their performance, ultimately leaving you feeling worse and potentially damaging the relationship you have with your children. If your sense of self-worth were to depend on a variety of factors, you might still feel pained by your children's setbacks, though to a lesser degree. Once again, the more you scrutinize and obsess, the worse you feel.

Living Flexibly

When food and weight dominate your focus, you inevitably struggle. We have only so much attention, time, and energy. When you immerse yourself in work, your social life may falter; when your focus becomes your appearance, you may lose sight of other elements of living.

A client of mine, Hailey, who is recovering from a serious history of anorexia, struggles with eating for emotional reasons. She made the transformative decision to choose living freely over living as a slave to food and her body. While she is in recovery, she occasionally faces urges and thoughts that she capitulated to in the past. Her best friend recently began to diet and started obsessing about her food, calling Hailey to review her calories and plan her meals. In her preoccupation with food, Hailey's friend fails to notice that the woman she is calling to discuss calories and sizes spent years in the hospital for problems with food. Of course she means no harm, and her asking Hailey is mindless, not malicious. All too often, a narrow focus may get in the way of the wisdom that arises from a flexible, broad awareness—which is more like a camera that can shift focus to capture an expansive view.

I really enjoy seeing my clients' pie charts. Sometimes they draw elaborate pictures or make collages. These can really highlight the difference of a move from body or weight obsession toward other values and priorities, such as loving animals or connecting with your British heritage (picture a pie slice with pictures of the latest royal wedding and Burberry plaid or, more seriously, family photographs). If it helps you, you may keep your life chart—the pie that reflects what you are moving toward—somewhere accessible to reflect and remind you of what matters most to you or what you would like to matter most to you.

Valuing

Over my years of seeing clients, I have noticed that the mixture of hopelessness and guilt is one of the greatest sources of pain people experience. There is so much we have no control over. But while we may not choose what we get in this uncertain world, we do get to choose what we contribute. Knowing in detail what matters to you provides your whole life with direction, hope, and clarity. While you may not be able to govern your weight, you may choose to pursue meaningful actions and construct both a new course of life and a method of evaluating it.

As we address values in this chapter, there is no assumption that you're *not* living according to your values. Rather, the main purpose in bringing awareness to your values is to clear away obstacles—namely feelings, thoughts, and actions—that may get in the way of living with intention.

Take a few minutes to honestly consider what matters to you, as you did earlier in the chapter. Now, rather than jotting down values or thinking abstractly, try to really *taste* these values. For example, if you value spirituality, you may envision in detail what it would look like to practice living with this value in your life. Mindfully notice the thoughts and feelings that arise in this process.

Exercise: Funeral Meditation

I'd like to begin this exercise in an unconventional manner. I'd like to ask you for permission, as this exercise may create a feeling of vulnerability. If you are willing, continue; if that feels too unsafe, you may skip over the exercise. In this meditation, allow yourself to feel, rather than thinking theoretically. You don't need to write just yet; instead, immerse yourself in this experience— you may write later.

1. Imagine that your life has ended and you are able to observe your own funeral. Consider:

    *   What do you want your life to symbolize?

    *   What would your tombstone say?

    *   How would you want specific people in your life to remember you?

    *   What exactly would you want people to say about you? How might friends memorialize you? Family? Your partner? How might people look as they spoke about you?

    *   How might your obituary read?

2. Notice thoughts that arise in this process, as well as feelings in your body.

3. Return to noticing what you ideally would like your life to stand for. In this process, you may imagine yourself pursuing certain ideal activities people may reflect upon.

4. When you are ready, bring your attention back to the present moment.

5. Consider for several minutes how your life resembles how you would like to live. Notice where you find yourself less active than you would like in areas that you know matter.

6. What do you notice as you reflect on what you want your life to stand for?

7. In all of this, how important was your appearance?

(Adapted from Hayes and Smith 2005)

♥

Before writing the above exercise, I took time to participate in this meditation. This morning it feels challenging to imagine my funeral, but I can clearly envision others living the values that I aspire to enact. I see in detail my grandpa, Emil, speaking with patience, humility, and focus. I see my grandma Sylvia connecting with kindness, placing herself in the background and others in the foreground. She never speaks harshly about another person or complains. She practices gratitude. I see their warm, generous faces. I notice their gestures and hear their words. Then I see myself and notice tendencies to fill silence with noise or rush from activity to activity. When I am mindless or stuck in habit, I assume that my value is in productivity. Upon reflection, I grasp that my value is actually in my commitment to slowing down and really showing up with sincerity, humility, and patience. My value is in mindful speech, not hurried words. These values relate to relationships with friends and family and to spirituality. I want my words to serve a spiritual purpose.

And awareness of my values brings up anxiety. I face the worry that I won't follow through; I notice sadness for where I am and for where my BlackBerry has been. I am willing to feel these feelings in the service of practicing living according to my values. I am far from perfect, but it's helpful to have a clear map as my guide. Persistence in and commitment to our values is a challenge we all face; we'll address this in more detail below.

Understanding Values

What are *values*, exactly? Values are life directions we choose. Your values reflect what you want your life to stand for, or your life's purpose. Values are neither social norms nor judgments about what should matter. Values arise from your inner wisdom. Values are reflected in actions more than in feelings. The following exercise will help you identify what you value and how you are experiencing your values in your life. Make more than one photocopy of the chart below to keep track over time of which values matter in your life and how you feel about your activity within each domain.

Exercise: Keeping Track of Values

The following chart lists twelve areas of life that are valued by many people. We are concerned with your quality of life in each of these areas, and for each there are several aspects you're asked to rate. Ask yourself the following questions when you make ratings in each area, being aware that not everyone will value all of these areas or value all areas the same. Rate each area according to your own personal view of it. You may find it useful to bring your attention to really feeling what the value tastes like, rather than studying this list in a technical sense. You may consider what you wish might occur in each of these areas. Please take your time and fill out this chart with a quality of mindfulness and acceptance of all that you notice.

Possibility: How possible is it that something very meaningful could happen in this area of your life? Rate how possible you think it is on a scale of 1 to 10, with 1 meaning that it is not at all possible and 10 that it is very possible.

Current importance: How important is this area in your life? Rate the importance on a scale of 1 to 10, with 1 meaning that the area is not at all important and 10 that it is very important.

Overall importance: How important is this area in your life as a whole? Rate the importance on a scale of 1 to 10, with 1 meaning that the area is not at all important and 10 that it is very important.

Action: How much have you acted in the service of this area during the past week? Rate your level of action on a scale of 1 to 10, with 1 meaning that you have not been active at all with this value and 10 that you have been very active with this value.

Satisfaction with level of action: How satisfied are you with your level of action in this area during the past week? Rate your satisfaction with your level of action on a scale of 1 to 10, with 1 meaning that you are not at all satisfied and 10 that you are completely satisfied with your level of action in this area.

Concern: How concerned are you that this area will not progress as you want? Rate your level of concern on a scale of 1 to 10, with 1 meaning that you are not at all concerned and 10 that you are very concerned.

	Possibility	Current Importance	Overall Importance	Action	Satisfaction with Action	Concern
1. Family (other than your partner or children)						
2. Marriage/partner/ intimate relationship						
3. Parenting						
4. Friends/social life						
5. Work						
6. Education/training						

7. Recreation/fun					
8. Spirituality					
9. Community life					
10. Physical self-care (diet/exercise/sleep)					
11. Environment (caring for the planet)					
12. Aesthetics (art, music, literature, beauty)					

Please take a few moments to consider your responses. What do you notice when you review your level of possibility? If a value matters to you and you are caught in unhelpful stories or a low sense of possibility is getting in the way of your moving forward, can you commit to act anyhow? If you notice that a value matters and you feel unsatisfied with the way you are moving toward what you care about, consider feasible steps you might pursue. When we talk about values, the focus is on living in accordance with our values. If a value is a theoretical idea, rather than a guide for action, are you really living the life you choose?

(Adapted from K. Wilson and DuFrene 2009)

♥

Virtues and Values

Virtues describe a set of moral standards that can guide us in *how* we implement our values. For example, if you value connecting with your family, you may further clarify that you want to connect with your family with *patience*. Or you may discern that you want to bring *self-direction* to your work. Virtues give our values-based actions detail. When someone offers a gift, we appreciate it more when the details reflect thoughtfulness—we feel a difference between receiving a gift card and being presented in a heartfelt manner with a more personal token. Similarly, in living, we may add meaning by noticing what matters and attending to the particulars. To get where you want to go, you need precision.

Here are some examples of virtues that may inform how we live according to our values:

- Humility
- Self-reliance
- Mindfulness
- Moderation
- Flexibility
- Loyalty
- Generosity
- Determination

- Service
- Compassion
- Self-direction
- Self-respect

- Nonviolence
- Love
- Faith
- Patience

Our virtues color our values, but a practice of cultivating any of these virtues (among others) can be a value in itself.

Goals vs. Values

It's easy to confuse goals with values. We learn to measure achievement according to outcome. When we focus on values, we let go of measurements and focus on living with virtue. Values are associated with an ongoing, active process. Goals resemble a to-do list. Certainly, our goals may relate to our values. For example, if you value living with kindness, you may make it your goal to find a volunteer activity. Notice, however, that showing up to volunteer does not necessarily mean you practiced kindness. Also, if you really value kindness, you might choose to extend your actions beyond volunteering periodically.

Values and virtues reflect why—and how—you show up; goals are where you hope to arrive (and virtues are how you get there). When we practice living according to our values, we have a different quality of attention than when we focus on our goals. For example, you may show up in class to learn (value) while you aim to earn a good grade (goal). If your value is learning, you may choose a course that is difficult, and you may not necessarily earn a top grade. If you are goal-oriented and your goal is excellent grades, you might avoid the more difficult class. Your focus shifts, and your choices may shift too. If you value health and your goal is to lose weight, you might not experiment with risky diets. You also may think about health on a larger scale rather than narrowly defining it in terms of your weight goal. You may commit to actions consistent with the larger value of health, such as seeking medical care and facing appointments and tests with willingness.

Emotional Wishes vs. Values

So often, in talking about values, people insist they want to feel happy, attractive, confident, or relaxed. We live in a "Don't worry, be happy!" big yellow ☺ culture, which may lead us into what Russ Harris (2008) calls the "happiness trap," the assumption that happiness is normal and achieved by chasing fun and running from pain. In fact, the word "happiness" stems from the root word *hap*, defined as "by chance." You can't get happy on purpose and stay that way any more than you can force confidence in a sustainable way. Spending a lot of money, sleeping in, taking lavish vacations, having casual sex, and using substances or food may lead to a feeling of happiness. Do these behaviors result in enduring happiness? Reflect on your own experience. Aspiring to attain feelings of happiness, attractiveness, confidence, or calm are examples of flimsy goals, based on emotional wishes rather than enduring values.

A more sustainable plan for living includes cultivating acceptance of your current experience and choosing to take effective action in a direction that may not prove "fun" but that is genuine in terms of what you actually want. As a wise person once said, "The main thing is to keep the main thing the main thing!" If your value is to connect, and you get caught up in worries about your worthiness, keeping the main thing the main thing entails purposely pursuing activities wholeheartedly, even at the risk of discomfort. Comfort is a narrow and precarious objective. There is no guarantee you'll find comfort even in staying home.

Valued Living Requires Skill

Living a *valued life*—that is, a life informed by your values—entails willingness to experience negative emotions in the service of your values. You may use any number of the skills addressed in earlier chapters, including accessing wise mind, urge surfing, noticing thoughts, acting opposite, tolerating distress, practicing self-compassion, coping ahead, and building mastery, to help you move toward what matters. For example, if you value learning and find yourself struggling and frustrated, living with this value includes persevering, sitting with urges to give up, noticing thoughts and feelings to eat and distract, and continuing to learn even in the presence of anxiety and frustration. It may feel more comfortable to live according to your values in times of ease; for example, learning something that is easy to grasp when you have time. To live according to your values during trying times requires devotion and skill.

Sorting Out Conflicts among Values

In addition to clarifying our values, we also need to develop a sense of priority among our values. We each have choices to make about what truly matters to us. At times, our values conflict with one another. A common struggle many people face relates to balancing productivity at work with participating meaningfully in relationships. The challenge is to make decisions about what matters mindfully from a place of inner wisdom. This takes time and experimentation, as well as acceptance of the fact that the elements of a fulfilling balance will shift over the course of our lives.

Procrastination Differs from Valued Living

Procrastination involves putting off valued living in order to do something sort of pleasant or to avoid difficult feelings. It makes good sense that we do this, when you think about how naturally we seek pleasure and avoid pain. In earlier chapters, we explored how pursuits like eating reward us on multiple levels, both adding positive emotions and taking away negative emotions. Yet, postponing valued living may mean we're dropping opportunities. Since we can never know how much time we have or how often certain opportunities will present themselves, procrastinating can hinder living according to our values. Equally important, it can maintain a cycle of training our minds to seek pleasure at the potential expense of meaning. You may not feel better the moment you move toward your values; however, you are guaranteed to feel worse over time if you *don't* move toward them.

Valued Living: Difficult and Meaningful

Thinking about what really matters to you can produce anxiety or sadness *at the same time* it facilitates creating a rich life that you choose. Clear awareness of what you care about often creates a sense of vulnerability; negative emotions may arise. Perhaps imagining in full detail a career that matters to you brings up thoughts and feelings related to anxiety: "I don't have the money for more training"; "If I pursue this fully, people will catch on that I'm a fraud."

Again, valued living may not feel as enjoyable in the short term. Even if you value kind speech, it can feel easier to gossip than to sit with uncomfortable silence and urges. Even when your value is faithfulness, cheating on your spouse may bring pleasure. Interacting lovingly with family members in trying circumstances is not exactly fun. Eating in moderation can expose your emotional hunger.

Just as a pregnant woman may cope with nausea and discomfort by envisioning cuddling with a smiling baby, when you are trying to live according to your values in the midst of experiencing difficult emotions, it may be useful to bring your attention to a more holistic view of your life. The following exercise will help you problem solve around the obstacles that tend to come up as you try to live your values.

Exercise: Committing to Valued Living

1. Reflect on some of the areas of valued living you've identified in your pie chart or during the funeral meditation.

2. Notice what sorts of thoughts, feelings, or behaviors tend to get in the way of your living in tune with what you care deeply about. To do this, imagine yourself in a familiar situation where it is difficult to act on your values, and notice exactly what arises. Imagine watching yourself and pausing at certain points, as you'd pause a film at a frame you want to examine in detail.

3. What thoughts and feelings do you expect to arise at these moments in the situation?

4. Next, generate a detailed plan for moving toward your values, with awareness of what may get in the way both emotionally and logistically. You may use skills you've learned earlier in this book as well as approaches that have previously helped you move forward in a meaningful manner.

5. What do you notice as you commit to pursuing a valued action by making a concrete and detailed plan to do so?

It is helpful to break down a commitment to valued living into specific and feasible steps. The purpose of commitment is not to get stuff done, but to move toward what matters even when your thoughts and feelings tend to move you away. When challenges come up, they give you an opportunity to solidify your commitment.

♥

Remember, practicing coping ahead exercises the same parts of the brain as actually engaging in the behavior. In order to move from habit to deliberate action, we need to slow down to bring awareness to our routine and consider ways to implement specific changes.

You might notice how moving forward actually feels as compared to how you anticipated it would feel before engaging. If negative thoughts and feelings arise when you pursue what matters, does the intrinsic meaning in fulfilling a valued goal feel worthwhile regardless?

Getting Support

Following through on what matters can feel challenging, and finding support can be instrumental. I know several people who have "gratitude buddies" with whom they share daily gratitude lists. What would it be like to start each day with an e-mail from someone giving you an authentic reminder to shift your attention to what's right? Personally, I know I wouldn't practice yoga as often if I didn't have my yoga community, and I have found that organized prayer and meditation groups similarly foster my practice.

Don't let logistics get in the way of what you care about. Get creative about ways to both connect with support and move forward with what you value. You might find resources online. Several of my clients who have mobility impairment enjoy taking university courses on the Internet.

If you are someone who works best when you are accountable, you may experiment with joining StickK (www.stickk.com), a website created by Yale University economists who observed the way commitment contracts increase success. StickK allows you to publicly commit to a goal. If you don't meet your goal, you can choose between giving money to a friend or a charity you choose. If you value productivity and charity, you win either way!

When you move from external, precarious goals (e.g., weight, food, fame) to a focus on values and values-related actions, you will actually set yourself up for feeling capable and purposeful. Wouldn't that be a crazy and wonderful thing?

Summary

Our problems are important, but living is more important. You can spend a great deal of time harping on your flaws and failing to appreciate your life. So much of this book emphasizes acceptance rather than control; values are a domain where you can practice flexible control, accepting your thoughts and feelings at the same time as you commit to pursuing values related to your actions. Here we explored what values are (life directions we choose) and are not (goals or emotional wishes) and how they relate to virtues. You worked through a couple of exercises to help identify what your particular values are and to make practical plans to move closer to living in accordance with them. "In this very moment, will you accept the sad and the sweet, hold lightly stories about what's possible, and be the author of a life that has meaning and purpose for you, turning in kindness back to that life when you find yourself moving away from it?" (K. Wilson and DuFrene 2010, 152)

Chapter 10

ENDING WELL AND BEGINNING AGAIN

We either make ourselves miserable or we make ourselves strong. The amount of work is the same.

—CARLOS CASTANEDA

A challenge we all face in making changes is how to maintain our gains and prevent relapsing into old ways. Fear of relapse can make us rigid, and can actually contribute to relapse. In this chapter, we'll discuss concepts and skills that can help you move away from "yo-yo" diets and rigid or temporary solutions, toward sustainable values-based choices.

One of the most powerful tools for sustaining change is the willingness to begin anew, again and again, with mindfulness and acceptance. Given that both food and feelings are constants in life, you will face temptations and you will experience slips. This is certain, and it is by no means a poor reflection on you or a bad thing in itself. One of the best predictors of successful smoking cessation is the number of previous failed attempts; in other words, trying to quit repeatedly means you are more likely to succeed. The thought "I can't; I've tried for years," is unsubstantiated by this research, since the person trying to quit smoking for the fourth time is more likely to succeed than a person who is on her first attempt.

When we see each moment as a time to begin again, moments generate exciting choices. One of the most important moments is when you notice that you've moved away from what you value—that is the moment to practice mindfulness, acceptance, mastery, and compassion. Formula 409, the ubiquitous cleaning agent, is called Formula 409 because it was devised on the 409th trial. Wipe your slate clean and give yourself room to start again.

"Problems" Are Opportunities

When you face a setback, take a moment to nondefensively and nonjudgmentally learn from the setback. A scientific way to change behavior in this nonjudgmental spirit is through *behavior analysis*. In this systematic approach, you specify a behavior you wish to modify, determine the causes of the behavior, and identify the potential challenges in implementing change. Instead of approaching a problem by fast-forwarding through it or avoiding facing it, which obscure detail, think of this method as hitting pause. Slowing down, you carefully examine the intricacies of factors underlying your behavior—external events, emotions, thoughts, and sensations—to gather important information that will help you move forward (Linehan 1993a). You can do this examination right away after a setback or at a later time when you have some perspective.

As an example of using behavior analysis, let's say you are repeatedly late. You can either get caught in shame and worry about this or use that same mental energy to thoroughly uncover the factors in the behavior. (In this case it might be best to notice the nuances related to this behavior once you're settled at work rather than as you run through the door, panic-stricken.) When you slow down and deliberately examine the behavior, you might note the following events, actions, and circumstances:

- Felt anxious and went to bed late

- Hit the snooze button

- Had the thought "It's okay if I'm a little late"

- Checked e-mail

- Spent time making wardrobe choices

- Noticed feeling fat and thought, "Changing clothes won't take long"

- There was a line at the café where I buy coffee

- Saw my old friend at the café and stopped to talk

- Thought, "It's rude to rush away"

- Uncomfortable shoes slowed my pace

- Caught in traffic

In slowing down to notice the details, you generate more potential solutions than the overly simple "I shouldn't hit the snooze button." Upon reflection, you may notice such possible choices as:

- Reduce vulnerability by getting more sleep

- Cope ahead and choose outfit the night before

- Notice thoughts

- Surf urges to check e-mail

- Practice mindfulness around time

- Problem solve: explore alternate routes to work; build in more time; buy espresso machine

If you were to combine several of these solutions, you might really change your timing.

Catch Yourself Capitulating

One propensity you may notice is the urge to *capitulate,* or give in to a behavior, such as using food to cope, overeating, not accepting, or moving away from what you care about. Capitulating is not passive—it's actively deciding not to bother (Safer, Telch, and Chen 2009). For example, if you notice that you haven't lost weight and feel sad, you may think, "It's too late," or, "Screw this," and head over to your favorite bakery. Capitulating is really different from acceptance. It's willful and comes from emotion mind. What happens when you repeatedly capitulate? You may come to believe you "can't" or feel hopeless. In noticing that capitulating is a choice, you may bring awareness to urges, thoughts, feelings, and your values when you face a desire to capitulate. This moment is an opportunity to build a sense of resilience and mastery. You may keep track of the urge to capitulate in your behavior analyses.

Notice "Irrelevant" Behaviors

Apparently irrelevant behavior (AIB) is a term used to describe a behavior that initially seems irrelevant; only upon close attention do you notice that the behavior actually impacts the behavior you want to modify (Safer, Telch, and Chen 2009). To notice AIBs, you need mindful awareness. Returning to the earlier example of finding yourself late, an AIB you might notice is not wearing a watch. You might assume that you'll keep track of time with your cell phone. With considerate attention, you might notice that you don't check your phone as easily and as often as you might check a watch.

The following are some potential AIBs you may notice that relate to emotional eating:

1. Postponing a meal or restricting your food. In the moment, you may think restricting is a helpful strategy in losing weight. But in fact, you may notice that significantly restricting your food intake often leads to bingeing. Have you ever gone to a restaurant starving and noticed yourself diving into the bread basket?

2. Eating from a container rather than serving yourself a portion.

3. Deciding to "just have one."

4. Packing a bland lunch you know you won't enjoy. If you realize that packing something you dislike will lead to your ordering in a second lunch, choosing overly bland foods might be an AIB.

5. Overvaluing weight or shape. As addressed in chapter 9, although it may feel counterintuitive, the more you think about and attend to your shape and weight, the less you will succeed. This is an AIB if you notice that this state of mind is not working.

Exercise: Learning from a Setback

1. Bring to mind a recent incidence of a specific behavior you would like to change; for example, the most recent time you ate for emotional reasons or violated a personal value. Describe why this behavior is problematic (e.g., "Coming to work late affects my productivity and increases my anxiety and may get me fired").

2. Specify exactly what the problematic behavior was and when it occurred (e.g., "I was twenty minutes late Monday morning").

3. Review in full detail all the factors that resulted in the behavior. You may reflect on vulnerability factors, thoughts, feelings, actions, events, and sensations (e.g., "I was tired; I thought, 'I can be a few minutes late'; I felt anxious; I changed clothes twice; I saw a friend; traffic was bad; my heart was racing...").

4. Look at the list of factors. Do you notice capitulating or AIBs?

5. Alongside each factor, describe a few potential solutions. Create a plan with several specific steps that may help you change your habit (e.g., "Modify my sleep schedule; sign up for StickK (www.stickK.com) to keep track of lateness; remind myself, 'Being late is not workable'; buy instant coffee for the office; organize my closet; carpool to increase my chances of leaving on time; sign up for HabitForge (habitforge.com) e-mails to remind me to go to bed on time").

You may consider each behavior analysis as a rough draft as you work toward understanding and changing your behavior; you can revisit and modify it as you gather more information.

♥

Monitor What Matters to You

As this book comes to an end, what are your aspirations? If you were to set goals and practice coping ahead, how might you proceed? Purposefully pursuing your values requires commitment and a good plan. We've covered many concepts and explored many tools to employ. With so much new material, one of the most helpful methods to practice paying attention and building mastery is to *keep track* of what you did and how it went—mindfully, nonjudgmentally, and in a spirit of acceptance.

The goal here isn't to feel better or feel negative emotions less. In fact, you may feel negative emotions more as you practice awareness and acceptance. The goal is to live the valued life you chose. Achieving this will most likely mean you will be noticing—and keeping track of—both negative emotion and skillful action.

Many people find it difficult to remember events or emotions in detail. When in emotion mind, you may forget that you felt differently earlier. And in emotion mind it's also hard to consider all of the practices you've learned. Using a reminder list of tools learned and keeping track of using skills will help boost your practice.

On the pages ahead, there are several forms to help you in noticing and labeling emotions and in practicing skills introduced in earlier chapters (you may also find these forms on my site, drjennytaitz.com). There is also space for writing a brief general note on your day. As you self-monitor, notice and implement changes to practice moving toward your goals. For example, if you notice an instance of emotional eating, rather than beating yourself up, conduct a compassionate behavior analysis.

I warmly encourage you to try your best in experimenting with keeping track of what you choose. Do it for a while to see whether practicing these steps enriches your experience.

If the number of skills feels overwhelming, break it down: highlight five skills of your choice. You may also start at the beginning of the book, focusing on one or two skills to practice regularly and continuing to add a skill each week.

Feel free to get creative. Choose, experiment, and modify as you like. Create and commit to a system that works for you. One client of mine, an art student, created a color-coded system in a journal, designating a daily value such as patience. Or you may use software to keep track.

Monitoring will allow you to notice in detail how much you used a skill and also keep track of the intensity of your experience.

Each moment—and each day, and each week—is a chance to start again by accepting yourself more. Valued living is a lifelong journey that requires understanding and diligence, but the road is always right before your feet. There's no prerequisite for beginning and no punishment for faltering; we only begin, and begin again.

Exercise: Keeping Track of Skills Used

For each day of the week, take note of what skills you used. In the chart below, the names of some skills are followed by a word or two of guidance that will help you usefully describe your use of the skill. It may also help you to use numbers when noting which skills you used and how useful they were, as follows:

0 = Didn't think about or use

1 = Thought about, didn't use

2 = Tried to use but couldn't

3 = Used skill; not helpful

4 = Used skill; found somewhat helpful

5 = Used skill; found very helpful

	Mon	Tues	Wed	Thurs	Fri	Sat	Sun
Notice and Label Emotions (specify emotions and intensity on a scale of 1–10)							
Accept Emotions							
Practice Willingness							
Notice Emotional Eating (specify when and where)							
Practice Mindfulness							
Formally:							
Informally:							
Mindful Eating							
Breakfast:							
Lunch:							
Dinner:							
Snacks:							

Eat at Moderate Hunger, Stop at Moderate Fullness									
Notice Mind States (emotion, reasonable, wise)									
Reduce Vulnerability									
Add Positives:									
Build Mastery:									
Cope Ahead:									
Notice and Surf Urges									
Observe Thoughts and Catch Interpretations									
Distress Tolerance: Review Costs and Benefits									

Soothe											
One Moment at a Time:											
With Other Senses:											
Find Meaning:											
Contribute:											
Self-Compassion											
Notice Critical Thoughts:											
Practice Loving-kindness:											
Ask Clearly:											
Focus on Higher Values											
Notice AIBs											
Catch Capitulating											

Notes

Mon	Tues	Wed	Thurs	Fri	Sat	Sun

Final Thoughts

Do we really know what will bring us joy? At the start of this chapter, we talked about how you might learn from your setbacks, giving them real, productive value. The idea that struggle is bad is a common inaccuracy. Now it is time to consider some other inaccuracies.

We confuse our memories with our expectations. All too often, we allow our emotions rather than our inner wisdom to govern our behaviors. This leads us to repeatedly pursue "fixes" that don't actually fix anything (Gilbert 2005). We spend a lot of time imagining how things will be, salivating over potential food choices, and shunning scary feelings. And so easily we forget the larger perspective—that the deliciousness and the dreariness come and go.

We started this book noticing how lottery winners are not happier than accident victims and how a tolerance for the momentary cravings that arise when sitting with a marshmallow relates to long-term success. My hope for this book is that it illuminates why the marshmallow, the house in Maui, or the Oreo cheesecake get us all stuck. Focusing on these false fixes potentially stifles the wisdom in our emotions, jeopardizes our sense of mastery, and delays our taking valued actions. While false or biased memories may tell us otherwise, we can't stop our feelings, and filling ourselves with food in the attempt doesn't work and isn't sustainable. Learning to accept urges and emotions does more than shrink your waistline. Living your life with awareness and acceptance of this moment can facilitate authentic nourishment. And the good news is that the ability to slow down and live mindfully involves skill—it is not a fixed character trait. Anyone can learn it.

Unattainable goals and inflexible attachment to them make us miserable. We spend a lot of time ruminating on what is "wrong" with us and trying to fix it with our minds—using the same thought patterns and habits that have not worked before. Surrendering into present-moment awareness, acceptance, and habits of the heart may provide us with achievable emotional sustenance. To move away from emotional eating, move toward what you really care about, even if your thoughts discourage you.

This book has introduced a good number of concepts and taught you a variety of skills and techniques aimed at helping you learn to experience and manage difficult emotions that can get tangled up in food, eating, and body image. I hope you have found inspiration, insight, and some new tools to try. I also hope to convey the message that you are more than your body and negative emotions. You embody virtue, and my wish is that you make a practice of clearing away anything that keeps you from knowing that.

> I wish I could show you, when you are lonely or in darkness,
> the astonishing light of your own being.

> —HAFIZ

References

Adams, C. E., and M. R. Leary. 2007. Promoting Self-Compassionate Attitudes toward Eating among Restrictive and Guilty Eaters. *Journal of Social and Clinical Psychology* 26: 1120–44.

Allen, H. N., and L. W. Craighead. 1999. Appetite Monitoring in the Treatment of Binge Eating Disorder. *Behavior Therapy* 30: 253–72.

American Psychiatric Association. 2000. *Diagnostic and Statistical Manual of Mental Disorders* 4th Edition, text revision. Washington, DC: American Psychiatric Association.

Andrade, A. M., G. W. Greene, and K. J. Melanson. 2008. Eating Slowly Led to Decreases in Energy Intake within Meals in Healthy Women. *Journal of the American Dietetic Association* 108: 1186–91.

Anestis, M. D., E. A. Selby, E. L. Fink, and T. E. Joiner. 2007. The Multifaceted Role of Distress Tolerance in Dysregulated Eating Behaviors. *International Journal of Eating Disorders* 40: 718–26.

Antony, M. M., M. G. Craske, and D. H. Barlow. 2006. *Mastering Your Fears and Phobias Workbook*. New York: Oxford University Press.

Atienza, F. L., I. Balaguer, and M. L. García-Merita. 1998. Video Modeling and Imaging Training on Performance of Tennis Service of 9- to 12-Year-Old Children. *Perceptual and Motor Skills* 87: 519–29.

Badia, P., J. Harsh, and B. Abbott. 1979. Choosing between Predictable and Unpredictable Shock Conditions: Data and Theory. *Psychological Bulletin* 86: 1107–21.

Baer, R. A., S. Fischer, and D. B. Huss. 2005. Mindfulness-Based Cognitive Therapy Applied to Binge Eating: A Case Study. *Cognitive and Behavioral Practice* 12: 351–58.

Barnes, R. D., and S. Tantleff-Dunn. 2010. Food for Thought: Examining the Relationship between Food Thought Suppression and Weight-Related Outcomes. *Eating Behaviors* 11: 175–79.

Baumeister, R. F., C. K. Nuss, and J. M. Twenge. 2002. Effects of Social Exclusion on Cognitive Processes: Anticipated Aloneness Reduces Intelligent Thought. *Journal of Personality and Social Psychology* 83: 817–27.

Baumeister, R. F., and J. Tierney. 2011. *Willpower: Rediscovering the Greatest Human Strength*. New York: Penguin Press.

Baumrind, D. 1971. Current Patterns of Parental Authority. *Developmental Psychology* 4: 1–103.

Beck, A. T., A. J. Rush, B. F. Shaw, and G. Emery. 1979. *Cognitive Therapy of Depression*. New York: Guilford Press.

Beck, J. S. 2007. *The Beck Diet Solution*. Birmingham, AL: Oxmoor House.

Bishop, S. R., M. Lau, S. Shapiro, L. Carlson, N. D. Anderson, J. Carmody, et al. 2006. Mindfulness: A Proposed Operational Definition. *Clinical Psychology: Science and Practice* 11: 230–41.

Bohon, C., E. Stice, and S. Spoor. 2009. Female Emotional Eaters Show Abnormalities in Consummatory and Anticipatory Reward: A Functional Magnetic Resonance Imaging Study. *International Journal of Eating Disorders* 42: 210–19.

Borkovec, T. D., and B. Sharpless. 2004. Generalized Anxiety Disorder: Bringing Cognitive-Behavioral Therapy into the Valued Present. In *Mindfulness and Acceptance: Expanding the Cognitive-Behavioral Tradition*, edited by S. C. Hayes, V. M. Follette, and M. M. Linehan. New York: Guilford Press.

Bouchard, C. 1995. Genetic Influences on Body Weight and Shape. In *Eating Disorders and Obesity*, edited by D. Brownell and C. G. Fairburn. New York: Guilford Press.

Brach, T. 2003. *Radical Acceptance: Embracing Your Life with the Heart of a Buddha*. New York: Bantam.

———. Forthcoming. *True Refuge: Three Gateways to a Fearless Heart*. New York: Bantam.

Brickman, P., D. Coates, and R. Janoff-Bulman. 1978. Lottery Winners and Accident Victims: Is Happiness Relative? *Journal of Personality and Social Psychology* 36: 917–27.

Chödrön, P. 1994. *Start Where You Are: A Guide to Compassionate Living*. Boston: Shambhala Classics.

———. 1997. *When Things Fall Apart: Heart Advice for Difficult Times*. Boston: Shambhala Classics.

Covey, S. R. 2004. *The 7 Habits of Highly Effective People*. New York: Free Press.

Craighead, L. W. 2006. *The Appetite Awareness Workbook*. Oakland, CA: New Harbinger Publications.

Craighead, L. W., and H. N. Allen. 1995. Appetite Awareness Training: A Cognitive Behavioral Intervention for Binge Eating. *Cognitive and Behavioral Practice* 2: 249–70.

Creswell, J. D., B. M. Way, N. I. Eisenberger, and M. D. Lieberman. 2007. Neural Correlates of Dispositional Mindfulness During Affect Labeling. *Psychosomatic Medicine* 69: 560–65.

Crocker, J., and L. E. Park. 2004. The Costly Pursuit of Self-Esteem. *Psychological Bulletin* 130: 392–414.

Dunkley, D. M., K. R. Blankstein, R. M. Masheb, and C. M. Grilo. 2006. Personal Standards and Evaluative Concerns Dimensions of "Clinical" Perfectionism: A Reply to Shafran et al. (2002, 2003) and Hewitt et al. (2003). *Behaviour Research and Therapy* 44: 63–84.

Dweck, C. 2006. *Mindset: The New Psychology of Success*. New York: Random House.

Eifert, G. H., and J. P. Forsyth. 2005. *Acceptance and Commitment Therapy for Anxiety Disorders: A Practitioner's Treatment Guide to Using Mindfulness, Acceptance, and Values-Based Behavior Change Strategies*. Oakland, CA: New Harbinger Publications.

Eldredge, K. L., and W. S. Agras. 1996. Weight and Shape Overconcern and Emotional Eating in Binge Eating Disorder. *International Journal of Eating Disorders* 19: 73–86.

Evers, C., F. M. Stok, and D. T. D. de Ridder. 2010. Feeding Your Feelings: Emotion Regulation Strategies and Emotional Eating. *Personality and Social Psychology Bulletin* 36: 792–804.

Fairburn, C. 2008. *Cognitive Behavior Therapy and Eating Disorders*. New York: Guilford Press.

Feldman Barrett, L., J. Gross, J., T. C. Christensen, and M. Benvenuto. 2001. Knowing What You're Feeling and Knowing What to Do about It: Mapping the Relation between Emotion Differentiation and Emotion Regulation. *Cognition and Emotion* 6: 713–24.

Foa, E., and R. Wilson. 2001. *Stop Obsessing! How to Overcome Your Obsessions and Compulsions*. New York: Bantam.

Forman, E. M., M. L. Butryn, K. L. Hoffman, and J. D. Herbert. 2009. An Open Trial of an Acceptance-Based Behavioral Intervention for Weight Loss. *Cognitive and Behavioral Practice* 16: 223–35.

Forman, E. M., K. L. Hoffman, K. B. McGrath, J. D. Herbert, L. L. Brandsma, and M. R. Lowe. 2007. A Comparison of Acceptance- and Control-Based Strategies for Coping with Food Cravings: An Analog Study. *Behaviour Research and Therapy* 45: 2372–86.

Fox, J. R. E., and K. Froom. 2009. Eating Disorders: A Basic Emotion Perspective. *Clinical Psychology and Psychotherapy* 16: 328–35.

Frankl, V. E. 1959. *Man's Search for Meaning*. Boston: Beacon Press.

Fruzzetti, A. E. 2006. *The High-Conflict Couple: A Dialectical Behavior Therapy Guide to Finding Peace, Intimacy, and Validation*. Oakland, CA: New Harbinger Publications.

Gailliot, M. T., and R. F. Baumeister. 2007. The Physiology of Willpower: Linking Blood Glucose to Self-Control. *Personality and Social Psychology Review* 11: 303–27.

Galloway, J. 2001. *Marathon: You Can Do It!* Bolinas, CA: Shelter Publications.

Ganley, R. M. 1989. Emotion and Eating in Obesity: A Review of the Literature. *International Journal of Eating Disorders* 8: 343–61.

Gilbert, P. 2005. Compassion and Cruelty: A Biopsychosocial Approach. In *Compassion: Conceptualisations, Research and Use in Psychotherapy*, edited by P. Gilbert. London: Brunner-Routledge.

———. 2009. *The Compassionate Mind: A New Approach to Facing the Challenges of Life*. London: Constable Robinson.

Goleman, D. 1995. *Emotional Intelligence*. New York: Bantam.

Greenberg, L. S., and J. D. Safran. 1987. *Emotion in Psychotherapy*. New York: Guilford Press.

Greeno, C. G., and R. R. Wing. 1994. Stress-Induced Eating. *Psychological Bulletin* 115: 444–64.

Gross, J. J., and O. P. John. 2003. Individual Differences in Two Emotion Regulation Processes: Implications for Affect, Relationships, and Well-Being. *Journal of Personality and Social Psychology* 85: 348–62.

Gross, J. J., and R. W. Levenson. 1997. Hiding Feelings: The Acute Effects of Inhibiting Negative and Positive Emotion. *Journal of Abnormal Psychology* 106: 95–103.

Gross, J. J., and R. A. Thompson. 2007. Emotion Regulation: Conceptual Foundations. In *Handbook of Emotion Regulation*, edited by J. J. Gross. New York: Guilford Press.

Harris, R. 2008. *The Happiness Trap: How to Stop Struggling and Start Living*. Boston: Trumpeter.

Hayes, S. C., N. S. Jacobson, V. M. Follette, and M. J. Dougher, eds. 1994. *Acceptance and Change: Content and Context in Psychotherapy.* Reno, NV: Context Press.

Hayes, S. C., K. G. Wilson, E. V. Gifford, V. M. Follette, and K. Strosahl. 1996. Experiential Avoidance and Behavioral Disorders: A Functional Dimensional Approach to Diagnosis and Treatment. *Journal of Consulting and Clinical Psychology* 64: 1152–68.

Hayes, S. C., and S. Smith. 2005. *Get Out of Your Mind and into Your Life: The New Acceptance and Commitment Therapy.* Oakland, CA: New Harbinger Publications.

Hayes, S. C., K. Strosahl, and K. G. Wilson. 1999. *Acceptance and Commitment Therapy: An Experiential Approach to Behavior Change.* New York: Guilford Press.

Heatherton, T. F., and R. F. Baumeister. 1991. Binge Eating as an Escape from Self-Awareness. *Psychological Bulletin* 110: 86–108.

Hennenlotter, A., C. Dresel, F. Castrop, A. O. Ceballos-Baurmann, A. M. Wohlschaläger, and B. Haslinger. 2008. The Link between Facial Feedback and Neural Activity within Central Circuitries of Emotion— New Insights from Botulinum Toxin–Induced Denervation of Frown Muscles. *Cerebral Cortex* 19: 537–42.

Herman, C. P., and D. Mack. 1975. Restrained and Unrestrained Eating. *Journal of Personality* 43: 647–60.

Herman, C. P., and J. Polivy. 2004. The Self-Regulation of Eating: Theoretical and Practical Problems. In *Handbook of Self-Regulation: Research, Theory, and Applications,* edited by R. F. Baumeister and K. D. Vohs. New York: Guilford Press.

Hoffer, E. 1955. *The Passionate State of Mind: And Other Aphorisms.* New York: Harper and Brothers.

Jeannerod, M., and V. Frank. 1999. Mental Imaging of Motor Activity in Humans. *Current Opinion in Neurobiology* 9: 735–39.

Jobs, S. June, 2005. Commencement address. Speech presented at Stanford University, Stanford, CA.

Kabat-Zinn, J. 1990. *Full Catastrophe Living: Using the Wisdom of Your Body and Mind to Face Stress, Pain, and Illness.* New York: Dell.

———. 1994. *Wherever You Go, There You Are: Mindfulness Meditation in Everyday Life.* New York: Hyperion.

———. 2003. Mindfulness-Based Interventions in Context: Past, Present, and Future. *Clinical Psychology: Science and Practice* 10: 144–56.

Kaplan, A. 1985. *Jewish Meditation: A Practical Guide.* New York: Schocken.

Kazdin, K. E. 1982. The Separate and Combined Effects of Covert and Overt Rehearsal in Developing Assertive Behavior. *Behaviour Research and Therapy* 20: 17–25.

Keesey, R. E. 1995. A Set-Point Model of Body Weight Regulation. In *Eating Disorders and Obesity,* edited by K. D. Brownell and C. G. Fairburn. New York: Guilford Press.

Kelly, A. C., D. C. Zuroff, C. L. Foa, and P. Gilbert. 2010. Who Benefits from Training in Self-Compassionate Self-Regulation? A Study of Smoking Reduction. *Journal of Social and Clinical Psychology* 29: 727–55.

Killingsworth, M. A., and D. T. Gilbert. 2010. A Wandering Mind Is an Unhappy Mind. *Science* 330: 932.

Leahy, R. L. 2002. A Model of Emotional Schemas. *Cognitive and Behavioral Practice* 9: 177–90.

Leary, M. R., E. B. Tate, C. E. Adams, A. B. Allen, and J. Hancock. 2007. Self-Compassion and Reactions to Unpleasant Self-Relevant Events: The Implications of Treating Oneself Kindly. *Journal of Personality and Social Psychology* 92: 887–904.

Legenbauer, T., S. Vocks, and H. Rüddel. 2008. Emotion Recognition, Emotional Awareness and Cognitive Bias in Individuals with Bulimia Nervosa. *Journal of Clinical Psychology* 64: 687–702.

Lehrer, J. 2009. Don't! The Secret of Self-Control. *The New Yorker* May 18: 26–32.

Leith, K. P., and R. F. Baumeister. 1996. Why Do Bad Moods Increase Self-Defeating Behavior? Emotion, Risk Taking, and Self-Regulation. *Journal of Personality and Social Psychology* 71: 1250–67.

Leyro, T. M., M. J. Zvolensky, and A. Bernstein. 2010. Distress Tolerance and Psychopathological Symptoms and Disorders: A Review of the Empirical Literature among Adults. *Psychological Bulletin* 136: 576–600.

Lindeman, M., and K. Stark. 2001. Emotional Eating and Eating Disorder Psychopathology. *Eating Disorders* 9: 251–59.

Linehan, M. M. 1993a. *Cognitive Behavioral Treatment of Borderline Personality Disorder.* New York: Guilford Press.

———. 1993b. *Skills Training Manual for Treating Borderline Personality Disorder.* New York: Guilford Press.

Linehan, M. M., and E. Y. Chen. 2005. Dialectical Behavior Therapy for Eating Disorders. In *Encyclopedia of Cognitive Behavior Therapy*, edited by A. Freeman. New York: Springer.

Lutz, A., J. Brefczynski-Lewis, T. Johnstone, and R. J. Davidson. 2008. Regulation of the Neural Circuitry of Emotion by Compassion Meditation: Effects of Meditative Expertise. *PLoS ONE* 3: 1–10.

Lynch, T. R., J. Q. Morse, T. Mendelson, and C. J. Robins. 2003. Dialectical Behavior Therapy for Depressed Older Adults: A Randomized Pilot Study. *American Journal of Geriatric Psychiatry* 11: 33–45.

Marlatt, G. A. 1994. Addiction, Mindfulness, and Acceptance. In *Acceptance and Change: Content and Context in Psychotherapy*, edited by S. C. Hayes, N. S. Jacobson, V. M. Folette, and M. J. Doughers. Reno, NV: Context Press.

Marlatt, G. A., and J. R. Gordon (eds.). 1985. *Relapse Prevention: Maintenance Strategies in the Treatment of Addictive Behaviors.* New York: Guilford Press.

Martell, C. R., S. Dimidjian, and R. Herman-Dunn. 2010. *Behavioral Activation for Depression: A Clinician's Guide.* New York: Guilford Press.

May, G. 1982. *Will and Spirit: A Contemplative Psychology.* San Francisco: Harper and Row.

Mayer, J. D. and P. Salovey. 1997. What Is Emotional Intelligence? In *Emotional Development and Emotional Intelligence: Educational Implications,* edited by P. Salovey and D. Sluyter. New York: Basic Books.

Mayer, J. D., P. Salovey, and D. R. Caruso. 2008. Emotional Intelligence: New Ability or Eclectic Traits? *American Psychologist* 63: 503–17.

Mennin, D. S., and D. M. Fresco. 2009. Emotion Regulation as an Integrative Framework for Understanding and Treating Psychopathology. In *Emotion Regulation in Psychopathology: A Transdiagnostic Approach to Etiology and Treatment,* edited by A. M. Kring and D. M. Sloan. New York: Guilford Press.

Mischel, W., Y. Shoda, and M. L. Rodriguez. 1989. Delay of Gratification in Children. *Science* 244: 933–38.

Muraven, M., D. M. Tice, and R. F. Baumeister. 1998. Self-Control as a Limited Resource: Regulatory Depletion Patterns. *Journal of Personality and Social Psychology* 74: 774–89.

Neff, K. 2003. The Development and Validation of a Scale to Measure Self-Compassion. *Self and Identity* 2: 223–50.

———. 2006. The Role of Self-Compassion in Healthy Relationship Interactions. Paper presented at the 114th Annual Meeting of the American Psychological Association, New Orleans, LA.

———. 2011. *Self-Compassion: Stop Beating Yourself Up and Leave Insecurity Behind.* New York: Harper Collins.

Neff, K., Y. Hsieh, Y. and K. Dejitterat. 2005. Self-Compassion, Achievement Goals, and Coping with Academic Failure. *Self and Identity* 4: 263–87.

Nolen-Hoeksema, S., E. Stice, E. Wade, and C. Bohon. 2007. Reciprocal Relations between Rumination and Bulimic, Substance Abuse and Depressive Symptoms in Female Adolescents. *Journal of Abnormal Psychology* 116: 198–207.

Nolen-Hoeksema, S., B. Wisco, and S. Lyubomirsky. 2008. Rethinking Rumination. *Perspectives on Psychological Science* 3: 400–24.

Oldham-Cooper, R. E., C. A. Hardman, C. E. Nicoll, P. J. Rogers, and J. M. Brunstorm. 2011. Playing a Computer Game during Lunch Affects Fullness, Memory for Lunch, and Later Snack Intake. *American Journal of Clinical Nutrition* 93: 308–13.

Pearson, A., M. Heffner, and V. Follette. 2010. *Acceptance and Commitment Therapy for Body Image Dissatisfaction: A Practitioner's Guide to Using Mindfulness, Acceptance, and Values-Based Behavior Change Strategies.* Oakland, CA: New Harbinger Publications.

Purdon, C. 1999. Thought Suppression and Psychopathology. *Behavior Research and Therapy* 37: 1029–54.

Rawal, A., R. J. Park, and M. G. Williams. 2010. Rumination, Experiential Avoidance, and Dysfunctional Thinking in Eating Disorders. *Behavior Research and Therapy* 48: 851–59.

Rieger, E., J. Van Buren, M. Bishop, M. Tanofsky-Kraff, R. Welch, and D. E. Wilfley. 2010. An Eating Disorder-Specific Model of Interpersonal Psychotherapy (IPT-ED): Causal Pathways and Treatment Implications. *Clinical Psychology Review* 30: 400–10.

Sacks, O. 2007. *Musicophilia: Tales of Music and the Brain.* New York: Vintage.

Safer, D. L., T. J. Lively, C. F. Telch, and W. S. Agras. 2002. Predictors of Relapse Following Successful Dialectical Behavior Therapy for Binge Eating Disorder. *International Journal of Eating Disorders* 32: 155–63.

Safer, D. L., C. F. Telch, and E. Y. Chen. 2009. *Dialectical Behavior Therapy for Binge Eating and Bulimia.* New York: Guilford Press.

Salzberg, S. 1997. *A Heart as Wide as the World: Stories on the Path of Lovingkindness.* Boston: Shambhala Publications.

———. 2005. *The Force of Kindness: Change Your Life with Love and Compassion.* Boulder, CO: Sounds True, Inc.

————. 2011. *Real Happiness: The Power of Meditation. A 28-Day Program.* New York: Workman.

Sandoz, E. K., K. G. Wilson, and T. DuFrene. 2011. *Acceptance and Commitment Therapy for Eating Disorders: A Process-Focused Guide to Treating Anorexia and Bulimia.* Oakland, CA: New Harbinger Publications.

Schwartz, J. M., and B. Beyette. 1996. *Brain Lock: Free Yourself from Obsessive-Compulsive Behavior.* New York: Harper Collins.

Segal, Z. V., P. Bieling, T. Young, G. MacQueen, R. Cooke, L. Martin, R. Bloch, and R. D. Levitan. 2010. Antidepressant Monotherapy vs. Sequential Pharmacotherapy and Mindfulness-Based Cognitive Therapy, or Placebo, for Relapse Prophylaxis in Recurrent Depression. *Archives of General Psychiatry* 67: 1256–64.

Segal, Z. V., J. M. G. Williams, and J. D. Teasdale. 2002. *Mindfulness-Based Cognitive Therapy for Depression: A New Approach to Preventing Relapse.* New York: Guilford Press.

Siegel, D. J. 2010. *Mindsight: The New Science of Personal Transformation.* New York: Bantam.

Swann, W. B. Jr. 1983. Self-Verification: Bringing Social Reality into Harmony with the Self. In *Psychological Perspectives on the Self,* edited by J. Suls and A. G. Greenwald, Vol. 2. Hillsdale, NJ: Erlbaum.

Telch, C. F., W. S. Agras, and M. M. Linehan. 2001. Dialectical Behavior Therapy for Binge Eating Disorder. *Journal of Consulting and Clinical Psychology* 69: 1061–65.

Thich Nhat Hanh. 1998. *The Heart of the Buddha's Teaching: Transforming Suffering into Peace, Joy, and Liberation.* Berkeley, CA: Parallax Press.

Thich Nhat Hanh, and L. Cheung. 2010. *Savor: Mindful Eating, Mindful Life.* New York: HarperOne.

Thoreau, H. D. 1854. *Walden.* Boston: Beacon Press.

Tice, D. M., and E. Bratslavsky. 2000. Giving in to Feel Good: The Place of Emotion Regulation in the Context of General Self-Control. *Psychological Inquiry* 11: 149–59.

Vohs, K. D., and T. F. Heatherton. 2000. Self-Regulatory Failure: A Resource-Depletion Approach. *Psychological Science* 11: 249–54.

Waller, G., and S. Osman. 1998. Emotional Eating and Eating Psychopathology among Non–Eating Disordered Women. *International Journal of Eating Disorders* 23: 419–24.

Wansink, B. 2010. *Mindless Eating.* New York: Bantam Books.

Wegner, D. M. 1994. Ironic Processes of Mental Control. *Psychological Review* 101: 34–52.

Wegner, D. M., F. Quillian, and C. E. Houston. 1996. Memories Out of Order: Thought Suppression and the Disturbance of Sequence Memory. *Journal of Personality and Social Psychology* 71: 680-91.

Whiteside, U., E. Y. Chen, C. Neighbors, D. Hunter, T. Lo, and M. Larimer. 2007. Difficulties in Regulating Emotions: Do Binge Eaters Have Fewer Strategies to Modulate and Tolerate Negative Affect? *Eating Behaviors* 8: 162–69.

Wildes, J. E., R. M. Ringham, and M. D. Marcus. 2010. Emotional Avoidance in Patients with Anorexia Nervosa: Initial Test of a Functional Model. *International Journal of Eating Disorders* 43: 398–404.

Wilson, G. T. 1996. Acceptance and Change in the Treatment of Eating Disorders and Obesity. *Behavior Therapy* 27: 417–39.

———. 2002. *Mirror Exposure Treatment for Bulimia Nervosa.* Unpublished manual, Piscataway, NJ: Rutgers University.

———. 2004. Acceptance and Change in the Treatment of Eating Disorders. In *Mindfulness and Acceptance: Expanding the Cognitive-Behavioral Tradition,* edited by S. C. Hayes, V. M. Follette, and M. M. Linehan. New York: Guilford Press.

Wilson, K. G. 2010. "Appreciating People with Profound Developmental Disabilities (or Finding Myself on my Knees, in a Steamy Bathroom, Useful): A Story of Finding Myself Useful after Years of Darkness." *Living One Life* (blog), *Psychology Today*, September 5, http://www.psychologytoday.com/blog/living-one-life/201009/appreciating-people-profound-developmental-disabilities-or-finding-mysel

Wilson, K. G., and T. DuFrene. 2009. *Mindfulness for Two: An Acceptance and Commitment Therapy Approach to Mindfulness in Psychotherapy.* Oakland, CA: New Harbinger Publications.

———. 2010. *Things Might Go Terribly, Horribly Wrong: A Guide to Life Liberated from Anxiety.* Oakland, CA: New Harbinger Publications.

Wilson, T. D., and D. T. Gilbert. 2005. Affective Forecasting: Knowing What to Want. *Current Directions in Psychological Science* 14: 131–34.

Wisniewski, L., D. Safer, and E. Y. Chen. 2007. Dialectical Behavior Therapy and Eating Disorders. In *Dialectical Behavior Therapy in Clinical Practice: Applications Across Disorders and Settings*, edited by L. A. Dimeff and K. Koerner. New York: Guilford Press.

Zettle, R. D. 2007. *ACT for Depression: A Clinician's Guide to Using Acceptance and Commitment Therapy in Treating Depression.* Oakland, CA: New Harbinger Publications.

Zepeda, L., and D. Deal. 2008. Think Before You Eat: Photographic Food Diaries as Intervention Tools to Change Dietary Decision Making and Attitudes. *International Journal of Consumer Studies* 32: 692–98.

Zhang, X., G. Zhang, H. Zhang, M. Karin, H. Bai, and D. Cai. 2008. Hypothalamic IKKb/NF-kB and ER Stress Link Overnutrition to Energy Imbalance and Obesity. *Cell* 135: 61–73.

Jennifer L. Taitz, PsyD, is a clinical psychologist and director of the dialectical behavior therapy program at the American Institute for Cognitive Therapy in New York, NY. She is a certified diplomate of the Academy of Cognitive Therapy and is a founding board member of the New York City Association for Contextual Behavior Science. Her expertise lies in emphasizing simultaneous acceptance and change and providing tangible tools to help people get "unstuck" so they are better able to regulate their emotions. She has presented at conferences internationally on mindfulness and acceptance. Visit her online at drjennytaitz.com.

Foreword writer **Debra L. Safer, MD**, is codirector of the Stanford Adult Eating and Weight Disorders Clinic and coauthor of *Dialectical Behavior Therapy for Binge Eating and Bulimia*. Her clinical interests include working with patients who struggle with eating disorders and obesity, designing interventions for post-bariatric surgery patients, and using computer-assisted therapies to increase the dissemination of evidence-based treatments for eating disorders.

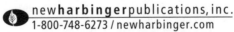